The Way of
TRUST AND LOVE

The Way of
TRUST AND LOVE

A Retreat Guided by St. Thérèse of Lisieux

JACQUES PHILIPPE

 Scepter

Other books by Jacques Philippe available from
Scepter Publishers

Time for God
Interior Freedom
In the School of the Holy Spirit
Called to Life

"My way is entirely one of trust and love."[1]

—Thérèse of Lisieux,
Letter to Father Roulland

---

1. LT 226.

Originally published as *La voie de la confiance et de l'amour*, copyright © 2011 by Editions des Beatitudes, S.C.C., Burtin, France.

Copyright © 2012, Scepter Publishers, Inc.
P.O. Box 211, New York, N.Y. 10018
www.scepterpublishers.org

Translated by Helena Scott

Text and cover design by Rose Design

Printed in the United States of America

ISBN: 978-1-59417-165-9

CONTENTS

KEY TO ABBREVIATIONS

The abbreviations used to refer to St. Thérèse's writings are:

— ms A, ms B, ms C: autobiographical manuscripts (published together as *The Story of a Soul* or *The Autobiography of a Saint* in various English translations). These references are followed by the page number of the original manuscript and r° (recto) or v° (verso). In recent editions of St. Thérèse's writings, the manuscript and page numbers are usually included in the text, so that quotations can be located easily.

— LT: Letters, with the number of the letter as given in the French edition of St. Thérèse's collected works, *Sainte Thérèse de l'Enfant-Jésus et de la Sainte-Face: Œuvres complètes* (*Textes et Dernières Paroles*), Cerf 1992. *http://bibliotheque.editionsducerf.fr/par%20page/2653/TM.htm#*

— PN: Poems, with the number of the poem as given in *Oeuvres Complètes*, Cerf 1992.

— Pr: Prayers, with the number of the prayer as given in *Oeuvres Complètes*, Cerf 1992.

— YN: "Yellow notebook" (last conversations), followed by the date.

INTRODUCTION

This book is based on a retreat that I preached in a parish near Madrid on the first weekend of October 2010, close to the liturgical feast of St. Thérèse of Lisieux.

In it, I tried to present the essential message of this young Carmelite nun, who died at the age of twenty-four and whom John Paul II proclaimed a Doctor of the Church in 1997. I wanted to explain what this "completely new little way," this "way of trust and love"[1] consisted of: the way that Thérèse discovered, followed, and then taught the novices in her charge in the Carmel of Lisieux. She foresaw that, far beyond that little circle of people, God also wanted to reveal this path to a legion of "little souls," weak, fragile people, to lead them to the very heights of love.[2]

Shortly before her death, Thérèse intuited that a huge task awaited her.

> I feel that I am going to my rest . . . but above all, I feel that my mission is about to begin, my mission of making God loved as I love him, of giving my little way

---

1. Thérèse also uses the expression "way of simple, loving trust." LT 261.
2. See the end of ms B.

to other souls. If God grants my request, my Heaven will be spent on earth, until the end of the world. Yes, I wish to spend my Heaven in doing good on earth.[3]

The wonderful way in which Thérèse's teaching spread, and continues spreading today, shows that her desire was not an illusion but reflected the wisdom of God the Father, who has "hidden these things from the wise and understanding and revealed them to babes."[4] In this as in so many other things, God was going to "surpass all her expectations."[5]

I did not think that the six conferences I gave in the course of that weekend should be made into a book, but I was asked if they could be published. Being unable to undertake a thorough revision of the texts, I have simply gone through the transcripts and tried to improve the style, clarify or complete some points, and add references and relevant quotations.

The result is certainly not perfect—it is still in a spoken style rather than a written one, and there are repetitions and digressions. Even so, it may help some people and, in particular, give them the desire to go more deeply into the message of the young Carmelite from Lisieux, which is, in my opinion, essential for the Church and society today.

---

3. YN, July 17, 1897.

4. Cf. Luke 10:21.

5. Cf. ms C, 3 r°.

In a vulnerable, wounded world like ours, where nevertheless the Holy Spirit is addressing all Christians with a ringing call to holiness and inspiring them with a desire to live out the Gospel message in all its depth, I think there is no better path than the one St. Thérèse of Lisieux offers us: her little way of trust and love. This book is best used, obviously, in accordance with its original intention, as the guideline for a retreat. For example, you could use it over the course of a week, reading one chapter a day and then taking time to meditate on it, re-reading the quotations in the context of your personal prayer, and asking yourself what light they throw on your own life, what invitations our Lord is making to you through them.

I.

A COMPLETELY NEW WAY

The main topic I am going to talk about is trust in God. The world we live in is not an easy one, and we sometimes carry, for different reasons, a heavy load of worries. It is therefore important for us to increase our trust; to ask the Holy Spirit for the strength of faith to be able to face up to everything we will have to live through in these times of ours.

When dealing with this topic, I sense strongly that God wants to create a new people and fill them with the strength of the Holy Spirit: a people who will be able to produce plentiful fruits for his glory, the proclamation of the Gospel, and the good of all mankind. This, however, is a people that includes little children and the poor. God's real strength is not mere human strength—it is not a matter of physical, mental, or intellectual abilities, useful though they may be. God's strength is made perfect in man's weakness, as St. Paul says.[1] We are invited to let ourselves be visited in our littleness, our poverty, our weaknesses, to receive a new strength: the strength of trust and faith.

The Church is going through difficult times. These difficulties, of course, are not the same in France as in Spain or in Pakistan, but we all face a definite spiritual combat. More than ever, perhaps, the Lord wants to give us his Holy Spirit, the Spirit that helps us in our weakness, as the Letter to the Romans says so beautifully.[2] It is he who teaches us to pray, introduces us into our true relationship with God, it is he who teaches us to believe, hope, and love. I am convinced that the Lord wants to do great things in our hearts. If you take the time to read this book prayerfully, with a heart open to God's Word, he will work marvels in you.

In the first five chapters of the book, I will comment on some passages from the writings of St. Thérèse of Lisieux, a saint who received a special grace to establish us firmly in the trusting attitude of small children. I shall talk about some of the lights received by St. Thérèse, which are still extremely valuable for us today. In the last chapter, I describe how to practice that trust amidst the difficulties and trials life brings. It's easy to

---

1. Cf. 2 Corinthians 12:9.
2. Romans 8:26.

trust when everything is going well, but when everything is going wrong, it's another matter! But still we must; and here we shall see how to do it, in a way that I hope will prove practical.

Thérèse of Lisieux—"Little St. Thérèse"—is perhaps less well known in Spain than "the great Teresa," St. Teresa of Avila. But she is a worthy daughter of the celebrated Reformed or Discalced Carmelites, with a vital spiritual message very relevant for today's world. Although she never pursued any theological studies, she was proclaimed a Doctor of the Church by Pope John Paul II on October 19, 1997, marking the centenary of her death.[3] The forthcoming proclamation was announced at the World Youth Day in Paris, where the relics of St. Thérèse were present. All of us, and especially young people, are invited by the supreme teaching voice of the Church to take lessons at her school.

I won't retrace our saint's life in great detail. She was born on January 2, 1873, and spent her childhood at Alençon and then Lisieux, in northern France.[4] We know that her childhood was marked by considerable suffering.

---

3. With St. Teresa of Avila and St. Catherine of Siena, she is the third woman to become a Doctor of the Church, and the youngest one.

4. Thérèse's parents, Louis and Zélie Martin, were beatified on October 19, 2008. They had nine children, four of whom died very young. All the surviving children were girls, with Thérèse the youngest. Four (Pauline, Marie, Thérèse, and Celine) entered the Carmelite convent at Lisieux, and Leonie entered the Convent of the Visitation at Caen.

She lost her mother to breast cancer at the age of four, and this left a deep wound in her. The bereavement was made worse by a series of separations, leading finally at the age of ten to a serious sickness from which she was cured by the smile of the Virgin Mary. These trials did not prevent Thérèse from developing great faith and deep love for God. Following a healing of her emotional fragility which she received on Christmas night 1886 at the age of fourteen, she found an inner strength that enabled her to enter the Carmelite convent as she desired at the age of fifteen. She died there very young of tuberculosis in her twenty-fourth year, on September 30, 1897.

After her death, as was often the custom among Carmelites, her convent published an obituary notice put together on the basis of Thérèse's autobiographical recollections (which she had written down at the request of her superiors), entitled *The Story of a Soul*. Unexpectedly, the book was a massive success, spreading rapidly around the world and touching many people's hearts. The extraordinary number of favors received by people who invoked her intercession also contributed to her reputation. For example, during the 1914–1918 war, before she was canonized (which occurred in 1925), many people, including soldiers, received special protection as a grace after invoking her. One of my uncles, a missionary among the Inuit in northern Canada, told me the mission was a total failure and they were on the point of abandoning it, when the bishop responsible for the mission traveled to Lisieux. He returned home with a little soil from St. Thérèse's grave which he scattered on the ground. Numerous conversions then began to occur. Thousands of stories like this could be told; the Carmelite archives are full of them.

Thus, St. Thérèse rapidly became very popular. Statues of her could soon be found in such diverse locales as New Zealand, Brazil, and the heart of China. She was canonized on May 17, 1925 by Pope Pius XI before 500,000 people, and was still more astonishingly proclaimed a Doctor of the Church by Pope John Paul II. In the judgment of the Church, she has become a primary reference point for us for understanding and practicing the Gospel message today.

Her style may not please some people, for it was very much in the manner of the nineteenth century, but her writings contain extraordinary forcefulness and truth. Pope John Paul II said Thérèse helps us rediscover the heart of the Gospel: the tenderness of God the Father, and the path by which we are called to become, in God's sight, like little children.

Of Thérèse of Lisieux, it can be said with conviction that the Spirit of God enabled her heart to reveal directly, to the men and women of our time, the fundamental mystery, the reality of the Gospel: the fact of having really received "a spirit of adoption as children that makes us cry out, 'Abba! Father!'" The "Little Way" is the way of "spiritual childhood." This way contains something unique that is part of the genius of St. Thérèse of Lisieux. At the same time it holds a confirmation and renewal of the most fundamental and universal truth. For what truth of the Gospel message is more fundamental and universal than this: that God is our Father and we are his children?[5]

In the Gospel one finds some very blunt words of Jesus: if you are not converted, if you do not change and become like little children again, you will not enter into the Kingdom of Heaven![6] Each of us has an absolute need for an inner transformation that makes us "as little as a child." What that means and how to put it into practice are exactly what Thérèse teaches in a simple, luminous way. That is why she was proclaimed a Doctor—that is, a teacher—of the Church. In this book I wish to offer some reflections on this topic that are quite simple but very valuable for our everyday lives in that they will help us rediscover the Gospel as "good news."

The Gospel is not a law that crushes us. Sometimes we may be tempted to think that people who aren't Christians are basically better off than we. After all, they can do as they like, while we have a whole list of commandments

5. Pope John Paul II, Homily at Lisieux, June 2, 1980.
6. Cf. Matthew 18:3.

to obey! But this is a very superficial way of seeing things. One of my great desires is that the Gospel always be presented as good news, happy news, filling our hearts with joy and consolation. Yes, Jesus' teaching is demanding, but Thérèse helps us see it as genuine good news, since the Gospel for her is no less than the revelation of God's tenderness, God's mercy toward each of his children, illuminating the laws of life that lead to happiness.[7]

The heart of Christian life is to receive and welcome God's tenderness and goodness, the revelation of his merciful love, and to let oneself be transformed interiorly by that love.

A passage from Thérèse's autobiography describes her main spiritual insight, which she calls the "little way." Aware of having a particularly deep perception of this Gospel truth, she desired to pass it on to the sisters she was close to in her Carmelite convent, especially the novices whom her superior had placed in her care. The sharing of this insight remained very restricted during her lifetime,

---

7. See the Letter to Father Roulland, LT 226: "Sometimes when I read certain spiritual treatises where perfection is shown through a thousand obstacles, surrounded by a host of snares, my poor little spirit quickly tires, I shut the learned book that makes my head ache and dries up my heart, and I take up Sacred Scripture. Then everything seems luminous to me, one single word reveals infinite horizons to my soul, perfection seems easy, and I see that it is enough to recognize one's own nothingness and abandon oneself like a child into God's arms. Leaving to great souls, great spirits, the beautiful books that I cannot understand and still less put into practice, I rejoice to be little, because only children and those who are like them will be admitted to the heavenly banquet."

but after her death her teaching spread in an extraordinary way. Shortly before dying, she said something that has become well known: "I wish to spend my Heaven in doing good on earth."[8] She is doing that today and will do so for each of us if we ask her to teach us her little way and make us love our loving God as she learned to love him.

So what is this little way? It is the spiritual journey undertaken by Thérèse, a genuine path to holiness, but a path accessible to everyone, so that nobody can get discouraged, not even the littlest, the poorest, or the most sinful—so that everyone can discover a path of life, of conversion, open to him or her. In this, Thérèse anticipated the Second Vatican Council, which stated firmly that holiness is not an exceptional path, but a call to all Christians, from which nobody can be excluded. Even the weakest and most wretched of men can answer the call to holiness.

This path of Thérèse's is given several different names in her manuscripts. She often talks about the "little way," as in the passage quoted below. She also talks about the "way of trust and love" or the "way of simple, loving trust."[9]

She made the discovery in successive stages, but the passage I wish to quote sums up the essence of that spiritual experience. It comes in Manuscript C, written in 1897, the year of her death.

---

8. YN, July 17, 1897.
9. LT 261.

She was writing to the nun who was her superior at the time, Mother Marie de Gonzague, who had authorized Thérèse to continue writing down her memories (at the suggestion of her elder sister), with the manuscript addressed to herself. This is what Thérèse said:

You know, Mother, that I have always desired to be a saint, but alas, I have always realized, when I compared myself to the saints, that there is between them and me the same difference as exists between a mountain whose summit is lost in the skies, and the obscure grain of sand trodden underfoot by passers-by. Instead of getting discouraged, I said to myself: "God could not inspire us with desires that were unrealizable, so despite my littleness I can aspire to holiness. It is impossible for me to grow up, I must put up with myself as I am, with all my imperfections; but I want to find how to get to Heaven by a little way that is quite straight, quite short: a completely new little way. We are in an age of inventions; now one doesn't have to make the effort to climb up a stairway in rich people's houses, because an elevator does the work much better. I too would like to find an elevator to lift me up to Jesus, for I am too little to climb up the steep stairway of perfection." Then I looked in the holy books for some sign of the elevator that I desired, and I read these words that had come forth from the mouth of Eternal Wisdom: "Whoever is

VERY LITTLE let him come to me" [Proverbs 9:4]. So I came, guessing that I had found what I sought. Wishing to know, O my God, what you would do for a little child who answered your call, I continued my search and this is what I found: "As a mother caresses her baby, so I will comfort you; I will carry you at my breast and rock you in my lap" [Isaiah 66: 13, 12]. Ah! never had such tender, melodious words come to rejoice my soul; the elevator that would lift me up to Heaven is your arms, O Jesus! To reach perfection, I do not need to grow up. On the contrary, I need to stay little, to become more and more little. O my God, you have surpassed my expectations, and I wish to sing of your mercies.[10]

Allow me to comment on this very rich text phrase by phrase. Thérèse begins with these words: "I have always desired to be a saint." It was true: ever since she was very small, Thérèse had wanted to be a saint. On one occasion, having already entered Carmel, she shocked one of her confessors, a Jesuit father, by telling him: "I want to be as great a saint as Teresa of Avila!" He felt that this indicated pride and told her to be content with being a good nun. But what the good priest took for presumption was in fact only the desire to respond fully to the Gospel call, "Be perfect as your heavenly Father is perfect,"[11] based on

---

10. ms C, 2 v°.
11. Matthew 5:48.

the confidence that God does not ask us for the impossible. And as we see, she succeeded! What matters now, though, is to understand how she did it.

Thérèse wanted to be a saint not out of ambition or vainglory, but in order to love God as much as he can be loved. That is completely in accordance with the Gospel. She also very much wanted to be useful to the Church, and she felt that the only way she could do that was by aiming for holiness with all her strength. But . . .

> But alas, I have always realized, when I compared myself to the saints, that there is between them and me the same difference as exists between a mountain whose summit is lost in the heavens, and the obscure grain of sand trodden underfoot by passers-by.

Thérèse very soon realized that what she wanted was impossible. Despite all her good will and her ardent desires, she was quickly brought face-to-face with her limitations and had the feeling that her desire for holiness was inaccessible, unrealizable. She felt as though there were the same distance between that ideal of holiness and what she could actually do as between a high mountain and a grain of sand. It should be said that at the time she lived, at the end of the nineteenth century, people still tended to identify the idea of sainthood with the kind of exceptional perfection that involved heroic enterprises, extraordinary graces, etc. Thérèse felt an insuperable distance between that model and what she was in her everyday life. Her words should be taken very seriously. She was faced with a real difficulty and unquestionably went through a real inner crisis.

The temptation in that kind of situation is discouragement: I'll never get there! How did Thérèse react? She goes on:

> Instead of getting discouraged, I said to myself: "God could not inspire us with desires that were unrealizable, so despite my littleness I can aspire to holiness."

Here is a very beautiful aspect of Thérèse's spiritual personality: her great simplicity, her trust in God. If God has put this desire in me—and I've had it for years, that's why I entered Carmel—then it must be realizable. The desire has always been with me. It can't be an illusion, because God is just in all his ways.

We are looking at one of the paradoxes of Thérèse's life: on the one hand, great psychological weaknesses and great sufferings; but despite this, on the other hand, always great desires.

Lest we idealize Thérèse, recall what she was like at almost fourteen, before the healing grace that came to her at Christmas 1886. She was a very intelligent little girl, but she had not followed a normal school life because she could not adapt to the school run by Benedictine sisters to which she had been sent. She was hypersensitive, very dependent on others, and had an enormous need for gratitude. When she had done some little act of service, such as watering the flowers, and no one thanked her, it was a full-scale drama for her. If by chance she had hurt someone she loved, she cried about it, and then, as she says, "cried for having cried."[12] "I was so oversensitive that I was unbearable." She was "enclosed in a narrow circle that she could not get out of."[13] Yet at the same time she had a very deep life of prayer and a true desire for holiness. It took the grace of Christmas 1886 to sort out this tangle, so to speak. I shall say a little about it here, and invite you to read the passage where she describes it.[14]

Briefly, then, after Communion at Midnight Mass, our Lord inspired Thérèse to make an act of courage to overcome her hypersensitivity. The youngest of the Martin girls, she was still treated rather like a child: at Christmas, there were gifts left for her by the fireplace, and so on. Their father, Mr. Martin, despite his affection for his youngest child, was beginning to be a little tired of all this. The comment escaped him, "This is the last time, luckily!" Thérèse heard this and it hurt her terribly; she was tempted, as usual, to cry like a child, which would have spoilt the whole family's Christmas.

---

12. ms A, 44 v°.

13. ms A, 46 v°.

14. ms A, 45 r°.

She tells how she received a grace at that moment which can be understood as follows. It was as if God made her understand, "That's it, finished." She received a sort of intuition, like a call from the Holy Spirit: "No, Thérèse, that childishness is over, you can't let yourself go and spoil Christmas for the others!" That is not exactly what the text says, but I think that's what it means.

So she made an act of courage: she acted as though nothing had happened, looked as joyful and happy as she could, unwrapped her presents with laughter and thanks, and, astonishingly, was cured from that moment on. She herself says she recovered the strength of mind she had lost at the age of four when her mother died, an event that traumatized her and lay at the root of all her emotional fragility. After that, she was able to enter Carmel and embark on her wonderful, courageous way of life, undertaking a "giant's race," as she puts it.[15]

I am telling you this to help you understand something: it may happen that God works a deep cure in us through totally insignificant events. Sometimes we are called by God to come out of ourselves, to take several steps forward, to become more adult and free. We turn round and round inside ourselves, enclosed in our immaturity, complaints, lamentations, and dependencies, until suddenly a day of grace arrives, a gift from God, who

---

15. ms A, 44 v°.

nevertheless also calls upon our freedom. We have a choice to make, for it is at the same time a cure and a conversion: our freedom has to opt for an act of courage. Making an act of courage even over some very small thing, which is what God is asking of us, can open the gate to in-depth cures, to a new freedom granted us by God.

We all need cures in order to become more adult in the faith, to be courageous in waging the battle that we must wage in the Church today. To be a Christian in this day and age is not easy. We will receive the courage and strength it requires if we can say yes to what God asks of us. So let's put this question to God: "What is the 'yes' you are asking me for today? The little act of courage and trust you're calling me to make today?" What is the little conversion, the door that opens to let in the Holy Spirit? For if we make it, God's grace will visit us and touch us in the depths of our being.

I am convinced that many of us will receive new strength from God. The door through which this strength enters us is the "yes" we say to our Lord to something he asks of us—something perhaps very small, perhaps rather more important, according as he gives us to understand.

I hadn't intended to stress that, but I think it is very important. We will come back to it again in the second part. At this point, let's return to the passage we were considering.

We saw little Thérèse facing this difficulty: she desired to become holy, but holiness lay beyond her capacity. Her reaction was to think: I cannot get there; I am tempted by discouragement. But no, I won't get discouraged, because God does not ask for what is impossible.

Recall another event from Thérèse's life. When she made her First Holy Communion at the age of eleven, she made three resolutions that I think are very good ones for us too. First: "I will struggle against my pride." (We shall see a little later what that means in practice when we talk about humility.) Second: "I will entrust myself to the Belssed Virgin Mary every day by saying the Memorare."[16] That's also a very good thing to do! Third, perhaps most important: "I will never get discouraged!"

So she wasn't discouraged, mainly because she was filled with confidence, sensing that her desires came from God, who is fair and could never inspire us with unrealizable ambitions.

A path toward holiness was, therefore, certainly possible, but she needed to find it.

The solution that might occur to us—"to grow up, to become great"—was discounted by Thérèse. "It is impossible for me to grow up, I must put up with myself as I am, with all my imperfections. I cannot change myself," she recognized. "I have to accept myself as I am, with

---

16. St. Bernard's well-known prayer to our Lady.

all my faults." We cannot change ourselves. We can make little efforts, but only God can really change us.

On this topic, we need to understand something else: we can't change other people either! Sometimes we wear ourselves out trying to improve others. It is better to accept them as they are.[17] And then a small miracle happens: when we accept them as they are, they begin to change little by little. That is the secret of living together, whether for families, married couples, or communities.

So the answer was not for Thérèse to grow up and become great, because she couldn't. There had to be another way. Where? She began her search, encouraged by the Gospel, which told her, "Everyone who seeks, finds!"

> But I want to find how to get to Heaven by a little way that is quite straight, quite short: a completely new little way.

Thérèse was not prepared to accept any old answer to her problem. What she wanted was, first of all, a way that was "quite straight." She could not be made to do a thousand complicated things; she needed straightforward things that would go directly to the goal. A way that was "quite short": she didn't want to waste time; she wanted to get quickly to the goal, holiness.

---

17. This does not mean we ought to refrain from taking any responsibility for forming others. But acceptance is the only basis upon which we can help someone else grow in anything.

Note, though, that achieving holiness takes a great deal of patience. Inviting one of those whom he was directing to develop patience, St. Seraphim of Sarov said, "Holiness is not a pear that is eaten in a day." But still we should aspire to find the quickest possible way to it, along which we can travel without wasting time or energy: one that goes directly to the point.

A little way that is "completely new." That is her most surprising expression. She has her nerve, this twenty-year-old who wants to find a new way to holiness after nearly two thousand years of Christianity! A new path to Heaven . . . that really is bold! How did the Church take to that? Had the theologians who pronounced in favor of Thérèse being made a Doctor of the Church actually read this passage?

The way Thérèse proposes is new on several counts.

In the first place, quite simply, she rediscovered the Gospel in its freshness and originality: the Gospel is always new. It is always good *news*, a new light. We get shut up inside our habits, routines, mistrustfulness, mediocre aims, and lukewarmness; in the face of all of that, the Gospel is always a new word.

Several of the psalms begin with these words: "Sing to the Lord a new song." That is surprising, because we repeat the same psalms, say these same words again and again. But sung with love, the song really is always new, because love makes everything new all the time. Love never tires. The

Holy Spirit can renew the love in our hearts every morning, as well as our faith and trust. The path discovered by Thérèse is a return to the novelty of the Gospel in contrast with our narrow-mindedness, our human limitations, our permanent blocks and hard-heartedness. The Gospel is always new: it always opens up new vistas, new and unforeseeable paths. We will never cease discovering the newness of the Gospel, because we will never cease discovering the ever-new richness of God's love and mercy.

There is a second sense in which this way is new, namely, by comparison with the mentalities confronting Thérèse even in the Carmelite convent. The piety of the nuns whose life she shared had many good elements, but there were also persistent traces of Jansenism, a difficulty in perceiving the goodness of God, a great emphasis on his justice, the severity of his demands, and, as I said earlier, a tendency to confuse holiness with certain extraordinary manifestations, which did of course sometimes occur in the lives of some saints (miracles, ecstasies, rigorous penances, heroic undertakings), but which are not the essence of holiness. This encouraged a tendency to exclude from holiness those we might call "ordinary people"—poor and little ones in particular.

Thérèse had the grace to restore the correct view of what holiness is, not the idea of it that people have sometimes made up, but what God really proposes to us in the Gospel, something accessible to everyone. As St. Paul says in the letter to the Ephesians, in Christ we all have free access to the Father.[18]

Finally, her way is new in a third sense: for her personally it represented a new phase in her life, a change of perspective, a sort of inner revolution that was immensely liberating. Thérèse had suffered for a long time from the fear that her inner poverty and imperfections were displeasing to God and separated her from him. She had carried a heavy load of worry about this, especially during her first years in Carmel, which were marked by great inner dryness and a keen sense of her limitations. At a certain moment when going to confession to a Capuchin father,[19] she came to understand that it was just the opposite: her "defects did not displease God" and her littleness attracted God's love, just as a father is moved by the weakness of his children and loves them still more as soon as he sees their good will and sincere love.

Thérèse went on to make a comparison that would help her discover her "completely new way."

---

18. Cf. Ephesians 2:18.

19. Father Alexis Prou. "He launched me in full sail onto the waves of trust and love that attracted me so strongly but onto which I had not dared to venture. . . . He told me that my defects did not displease God, that in his place he could tell me, speaking on behalf of God, that he was very happy with me." ms A, 80 v°.

We are in an age of inventions; now one doesn't have to make the effort to climb up a stairway in rich people's houses, because an elevator does the work much better.

As we know, in 1887 Thérèse went with her father and her sister Celine on a pilgrimage to Rome organized by the diocese of Normandy in support of Pope Leo XIII, at a time when the papacy had lately been stripped of the Papal States. The group consisted of about two hundred people, including sixty-three priests and bishops. Thérèse's main purpose in going was to ask the Holy Father for permission to enter Carmel at the age of fifteen. But in addition, this one great journey of her life was extremely rich in lessons for the future enclosed nun. It was on the pilgrimage that she discovered in particular her vocation to pray for priests. She knew them from a distance and idealized them; now, living in their company for four weeks made her realize "that they are in great need of prayer."[20]

The group visited the great cities of Italy—Milan, Rome, and others—and the big hotels where they stayed had elevators. Elevators had just been invented, and Thérèse and Celine were fascinated by this invention, which did not exist in Lisieux at that time. She goes on:

---

20. ms A, 56.

I too would like to find an elevator to lift me up to Jesus, for I am too little to climb up the steep stairway of perfection.

Where could she find this elevator? Where did Thérèse go to look for it? To the Bible.

This is worth noting. Thérèse had a great love for Holy Scripture. All the lights that guided her along the way, all her great spiritual intuitions, she found in Scripture. Every time a question came up that upset her a little, she went to the Bible to find the answer. She received astonishing lights that enabled her to acquire a deep understanding of the Scriptures. On this point too, she anticipated Vatican II, which laid great stress on the importance of returning to the Bible if we want to be real Catholics.

The Bible is not a privileged possession of Protestants: all believers, absolutely, must be nourished on Scripture. It is particularly vital for today, and we should ask St. Thérèse to obtain this grace for us. We live in a world with a lot of confusion and many contradictory messages. One need only turn on the radio to realize this. Depending on the station or wavelength, we can hear all the news in the world told in completely opposite ways. We are constantly bombarded with messages of every kind. Only God's Word, passed on to us in a special way in Scripture, has the necessary depth, clarity, and authority to help us find our way. Only Scripture enables us to discover the truth, not as something abstract, but as God's presence in our lives and the very specific way he offers us day after day.

True, Scripture is sometimes enigmatic and hard to interpret. However, if we spend at least ten minutes a day reading it, meditating on it, and praying about it (which, happily, many Christians do today), it will speak to our hearts. We should never let a day pass without taking some minutes to read and pray about a text from the Bible such as the readings for that day or a psalm. This faithfulness will be amply rewarded; from time to time we will have a wonderful experience. A particular verse that seemed obscure up until now, or that we'd heard a hundred times without its saying anything special, is suddenly lit up with a new light. And we'll exclaim, "These words were written just for me! This, and nothing else, is what I should be doing!" We are given, so to speak, proof and at the same time strength, and we see that this word is the light that is to guide us today; by putting it into practice, we'll receive life, we'll advance constructively and positively.

This simple spiritual experience of discovering Holy Scripture as light, encouragement, and strength for our path today—for Scripture has an authority possessed by no human word, no human reasoning—is one all Christians can and should have. We should live by God's Word and not content ourselves with what we hear on the radio and television. Some of those things are positive, but there are all sorts of things! Nor should we live off our impressions, feelings, imagination, and reflections. All of these are positive, but they can sometimes deceive us and in any case are not enough. We need the clarity and strength of God's Word or else we'll get lost in this world.

It is not always simple to be a Christian today. But God is faithful and the Holy Spirit is even now making us rediscover how strong a force the Word of God is in our lives. And also the Eucharist. Blessed John Paul II, in his wonderful writings, said that the further the Church advances in history, the more she is called to find her strength above all in Scripture and the Eucharist, both received in a climate of prayer.

I've been digressing a bit, but the point is fundamental. We can obtain many graces by praying to little Thérèse. Ask for whatever you want, but don't forget to ask for love for the Word, understanding of Scripture. Here's something I find really striking: St. Luke's gospel tells us that after the Resurrection the Risen Christ opened his disciples' hearts to understand the Scriptures.[21] What until then had been closed and incomprehensible suddenly became radiant with light. So let's ask St. Thérèse for love for the Bible, as well as for the spiritual understanding of the Scriptures that was such a great support to her. She

---

21. Cf. Luke 24:45.

never really had a spiritual guide. With a few rare exceptions, she never had the chance to open up to someone who really understood her. But through Scripture, prayerfully read, she discovered everything she needed.

> It is above all the Gospel that occupies me during my prayers. In it I find everything needful for my soul in its poverty and littleness. There I always discover new lights, hidden and mysterious meanings.[22]

---

22. ms A, 83 v°.

2.

AN ELEVATOR FOR
SMALL CHILDREN

L et's get back to our elevator. Thérèse desired to
 be a saint, she wanted to love with all her being,
but she was faced with her own limitations and her
inability to change by her own efforts. She wanted to
avoid discouragement, which is the main danger in the
spiritual life. Father Libermann, a Jew who discovered
Christ and then became a priest and a founding mem-
ber of the Holy Ghost Fathers, used to say: "Discouragement is the downfall of souls!" She needed to find
a little way, a new, simple way, of living the Gospel: an
elevator to take her to Jesus. Following the good habit
she had developed, she went to the Scriptures to look
for the answer.

She could have found it in the Gospel directly. After
all, there is a very clear pointer to such an elevator in Jesus'
words: "Everyone who exalts himself will be humbled,

but he who humbles himself will be exalted."[1] That text could have been her starting point. But she went to find it in one, or rather two, passages from the Old Testament.

Let's continue reading:

> Then I looked in the holy books for some sign of the elevator that I desired, and I read these words that had come forth from the mouth of Eternal Wisdom: "Whoever is <u>very little</u> [and Thérèse underlined these words] let him come to me."[2]

I'll make another detour here. I have spoken about Thérèse's love for Scripture, but we need to realize that when she was in the Carmelite convent, she never had a whole Bible available. At that time, it was not possible for a young nun to have one. Fortunately, she had her sister Celine, who had remained "in the world" to look after their father, who was sick. (She too would enter the Lisieux Carmel after he died.) She had been able to buy herself a Bible, complete with the whole of the Old Testament. When she came across particularly beautiful or striking passages, she copied them out and passed them on to Thérèse. Many of Thérèse's deepest intuitions are thus based on passages from the Old Testament that she had discovered thanks to her sister, to

---

1. Luke 18:14.

2. Proverbs 9:4. In modern Bibles the translation is often slightly different.

whom she was very close and had passed on her own love for the Bible.

It was the expression "whoever is very little" that really struck home. Who was the "little one" that Scripture speaks of? It was Thérèse herself, fired with a great desire for holiness but suffering over her own powerlessness, anguished to find herself so weak and small.

What was God saying to this "little one"? Not "You need to improve. I'm not happy with you—what you're doing isn't enough!" But the opposite: "Whoever is little, let him come to me! Don't be scared . . . come!" This is no other than the invitation "Come to me" that we find in the Gospel. "All you who labor, who are bent under the weight of your burden, who find the demands of the Law too heavy, come to me, for I am gentle and humble of heart, and you will find rest for your souls."[3] Thérèse continues:

> So I came, guessing that I had found what I sought. Wishing to know, O my God, what you would do for the little child who answered your call . . .

In response to this invitation, the little child came to God simply and trustingly. What would happen to her?

> I continued my search and this is what I found . . .

3. Cf. Matthew 11:28.

Thérèse then offers a second quotation from Scripture, a magnificent passage from Chapter 66 of Isaiah. It revealed what God would do for the little child, the person who wanted so much to be a saint, who saw herself as being so poor and imperfect and suffered over it, yet came to God anyway. Would God accuse her of her faults? No, he was going to console her:

> "As a mother caresses her baby, so I will comfort you; I will carry you at my breast and rock you in my lap!"

God was going to console her, telling her: "Don't worry, don't be discouraged by your weaknesses." We soon see why: "It is precisely through your weaknesses, in your poverty, that I will act with my power; what you can't do with your own strength, I will do." Thérèse did not say all this in the passage we are looking at; it's a summary of what she would explain elsewhere. But I believe that these were the mysterious words of consolation God addressed to her. "Instead of bearing your poverty as a handicap, an obstacle, accept it and welcome it as a grace."

This is her revolution, her novelty. It is at one and the same time a new way of looking at God and a new way of looking at ourselves, a way of reconciliation with ourselves in all our weakness and poverty. I'll come back to this later, because it's fundamental.

At this point, Thérèse contented herself with quoting the incredibly tender words from Isaiah: "As a mother caresses her baby, so I will comfort you; I will carry you at my breast..." Here at last was the longed-for elevator: God himself would pick her up and carry her, hug her to his breast and rock her on his knees.

Let's read what she says next:

> Ah! never had such tender, melodious words come to rejoice my soul; the elevator that would lift me up to Heaven is your arms, O Jesus!

This language is quite surprising, because the passage speaks of God as father and even mother ("as a mother caresses her baby"), and then Thérèse goes straight on to speak of "Jesus' arms." But this is a profound truth. God is one, Father, Son, and Holy Spirit; he has the same tenderness for the poor and for little children.[4]

So here is the elevator: Jesus' arms—the mercy of God who gives himself through Christ—are going to lift up Thérèse to what seemed totally inaccessible: real holiness.

She continues with a vitally important comment:

> To reach perfection, I do not need to grow up. On the contrary, I need to stay little, to become more and more little.

---

4. Dame Julian of Norwich, an English mystic of the Middle Ages, does not hesitate to speak of Jesus as "our loving mother"! *Revelations of Divine Love*, chapter 60.

If I want the elevator to come down for me and to be lifted onto God's lap, I need to remain little or it won't work. If I'm too big, too sure of myself, the elevator won't come down to me. . . . Not "big" in the sense of "adult": as I explained earlier, Thérèse had worked very hard to grow up, to be free on the emotional plane, to be courageous and determined. After the grace she received on Christmas Day 1886, the youngest of the Martin girls quickly became very mature, strong in the faith, and psychologically autonomous. There is no question here of childishness, but just the opposite.

Thérèse discovered that the ultimate secret she sought was that she did not need to become great or grow up; on the contrary, she needed to stay little, and actually to become littler and littler. She continues with a joyful song of thanksgiving:

> O my God, you have surpassed my expectations, and I wish to sing of your mercies.

To express her gratitude she once again makes use of the Bible, quoting from Psalm 71 (we will never find anything better than the psalms to express our praise):

> O God, from my youth thou hast taught me, and I still proclaim thy wondrous deeds. So even to old age I will proclaim thy might.

"For my whole life long, I will never stop singing of God's mercies. . . ." After these words, Thérèse passed on to another subject: how old would that "old age" be? How long would God keep her on this earth? But that was all she had to say on the subject that concerns us here. She was fully content; she had discovered that the essence of the "little way," the new way to holiness, was to stay little and to become progressively littler. And this approach was very definitely going to attract to her the grace of Jesus, who would act as her "elevator" and lift her up to where she wanted to be, to the very summit of love.

All the same, when we read this we are left somewhat unsatisfied. What does "staying little" mean in practice? Thérèse doesn't tell us here; she gives glimpses, but does not explain it as fully as we would wish.

Fortunately, she does explain it elsewhere. In fact, one might say that the main aim of all her writings—her auto-biographical accounts, letters, and poems—is to make us understand what this "littleness" consists of, and how we are called to put it into practice. Firstly, in our relation-ship with God: certain passages express what "being little" means in our prayer life, when, for instance, we are living through times of dryness and darkness. Then, in living with others: Manuscript C contains some magnificent chapters on community life in the Carmelite convent that are easily applicable to the life of any family. She also talks about how to practice the little way amid suffering and trials. In the two last years of her life she endured very painful trials indeed: the physical suffering of the tuberculosis that led to her death and at the same time an extremely black "dark night of the soul" that affected her faith and hope. Her testimony is extremely valuable, since it shows that her "little way" is not to be practiced only in ordinary situations but is also a viable resource in the worst of trials. And it can lead to heroic courage and self-giving.

Thérèse's line of thought is simple but at the same time very rich. She covers a whole host of subjects in her writings. She also talks about the mystery of the Church, the priesthood, the Eucharist, Mary, etc. In discussing all these topics, not systematically but quite simply with reference to the life she is leading, she makes us understand what "being little" is: the Gospel call to be converted and become like little children again is the only path to enter the Kingdom of Heaven.[5]

Thus what we need to do now is consider how to practice this attitude of littleness in the different areas of our lives. I can't cover all the aspects of this topic, and I invite you to read and meditate on St. Thérèse's writings for yourselves. But we are going to look at the themes that I think are really fundamental.

A little later on I will quote some words of St. Thérèse, noted down, with others, by her sisters during her last

---

5. Cf. Matthew 18:3.

illness, in answer to this very question: "What does being little mean?" Here she spelled out the main aspects of her idea of littleness.

But first, to throw light on the deep theological basis of her teaching, something needs to be pointed out.

Thérèse felt clearly that she could not become a saint through her own efforts alone. Her own merits or her good works could not save her. In this way she was simply agreeing with the message of the Gospel and of St. Paul: We are not saved by our deeds, by what we accomplish. We are saved by grace, by mercy, and this grace is received through faith and trust.

The fact that we can't save ourselves is something we acknowledge in words, but in fact we find it very hard to accept. We'd all like to be saved by our own efforts, to be strong and robust, to boast about our successes, to shine in other people's eyes, even on the spiritual level. Worldly people want to be highly regarded because they have luxurious cars, expensive watches, designer clothes, professional prestige, and go around with beautiful people. As good Christians, we may want to stand out for our virtues, charisms, experience, and sound judgment. Then we consider that we are on the right path. But in fact we're in danger of ending up with exactly the same mindset as the worldly people described above. Very often, without realizing it, we have a worldly outlook on the spiritual life: self-fulfillment, self-affirmation, expansion of ego, etc.

And spiritual pride, we must be aware, is sometimes more destructive than social, worldly pride.

We cannot be saved by what we do; we can only be saved by grace, when God's freely given love comes, takes hold of us, and transforms us, sometimes gently and progressively, but sometimes in a spectacular way. In general, the transformation is fairly slow and progressive, without our always being able to notice the action of grace.

We would like to feel that we're making progress, improving and advancing, and sometimes we do see it: we're aware that God has untied a knot, as he did for Thérèse that Christmas. But very often we don't feel anything. Yet God is still acting, and one day we will see the fruits. Like the seed the Gospel speaks of, a tiny little grain of mustard seed, God has secretly sown something in our hearts; then, whether we wake or sleep, the seed grows, bears fruit, and becomes like a tree in which the birds of the sky can find refuge.[6] These are the fruits of the secret working of grace for our benefit and our neighbors'; they grow by themselves, so to speak, and we end up seeing how the poor lost birds of today's world find consolation, hope, encouragement, acceptance, and tenderness with us.

So the underlying issue, in the human and spiritual life, is to discover (and practice) the inner attitudes, the

---

6. See the parables about the mysterious growth of the Kingdom, cf. Matthew 4:31–33 and Mark 4:26–29.

dispositions of heart, that make us permeable to God's grace and attract it unfailingly: small and poor, yet attracting God's grace in an absolutely certain way. Not because anyone can manipulate God. If anyone can't be manipulated, it's God. But he is faithful, and he loves us, and so we can find absolutely unfailing ways of attracting his grace.

Those ways are summed up by Thérèse in the notion of littleness. It is something she probably discovered through St. John of the Cross. She found rich nourishment in the writings of this great Carmelite saint. Although the two of them seem very different from one another, I would say that in certain aspects there is a greater similarity between John of the Cross and Thérèse of Lisieux than between Thérèse and Teresa of Avila. St. John says we can obtain everything from God if only we know how to take hold of him by love.[7] We must approach him in the right attitude—love—expressed mainly in humility and trust. Let's look at this in greater detail.

Humility, because Scripture says: "God opposes the proud, but gives grace to the humble."[8] And trust, because God has the heart of a father. A father cannot resist his

---

7. "Great is the power and tenacity of love, for it overcomes and binds God Himself. Happy the soul that loves, for she takes her God prisoner, obedient to all that she desires. For His nature is such that, if one takes Him by love and gets on the right side of Him, one will make Him do as one wants." (The Spiritual Canticle [ital], Stanza 32).

8. 1 Peter 5:5.

children's trust—he finds it impossible to hold out against it. Once someone has a father's heart, he's lost, unable to resist being conquered by the trust of a little child. If a small child says, "Daddy, I'm not perfect, I do lots of silly things, but you know how much I love you! And when I do something silly, I ask you to punish me with a kiss!"— how could any father resist?

These are Thérèse's own words, and this is the heart of her message, which is simply that of the Gospel. She invites us to rediscover, and put into practice, the right attitudes which will enable grace to reach us. Admittedly, putting them into practice demands patience and perseverance, effort and courage; but I would call it well-placed courage. Efforts to change ourselves are bound to fail; the courage we need is that of persevering in the kind of fruitful dispositions that open us up effectively to God's action.

Let's look at some of these attitudes. First of all, as an overview, I want to quote a passage in the Yellow Notebook, a collection of Thérèse's words compiled in the last months of her life by Sister Agnes of Jesus (her sister Pauline).

This passage is dated August 6, 1897, shortly before her death (which occurred on September 30).

> I asked her in the evening during Matins what she understood by "remaining little before God." She answered, "It is to recognize our nothingness, to expect

everything from God, as a little child expects everything from his or her father; it is not getting worried or
upset about anything."

Not getting upset about anything—doesn't Scripture
tell us, "Have no anxiety about anything!"[9]

"Not to earn a fortune."

Not to seek to accumulate merits, virtues, security. If we
have such things, that's great, but we shouldn't rely on them.

"Even in poor families, small children are given what
they need, but as soon as they grow older, their father
doesn't want to feed them any longer and tells them,
'Go out to work, now you can look after yourself.' It
is so as not to hear those words that I never wanted to
grow up, feeling incapable of earning my living—of
earning eternal life in Heaven."

That could be taken in the wrong way: a suspicious
psychoanalyst would hasten to accuse Thérèse of childishness and immaturity. But that would be the exact
opposite of the truth. I have already spoken of how courageously she struggled to achieve emotional autonomy and
how quickly she became very mature. Take an example
from the beginning of her religious life in the Carmelite

---

9. Philippians 4:6.

convent. She came from a warm and loving family, and as the youngest child was always surrounded with affection. In Carmel she had to accept a certain degree of loneliness. She was tempted to become too attached to her mother superior, a mother-figure on whom she could have become dependent. She tells how, a hundred times a day, she thought of things she could ask permission for, as an excuse for knocking on mother superior's door and so finding "a few drops of joy" with her. But she denied herself this opportunity, although sometimes the temptation was so strong she had to cling to the banister so as not to give in.[10] She realized that seeking human consolation in the company of Mother Marie de Gonzague was a trap that would have kept her immature and dependent.

On the human level, then, she made heroic efforts to become adult and free. But at the same time she understood that in the spiritual sphere, in what referred to her relationship with God, things were different. The more one grows in the spiritual life, the more one depends on God, lives off God, receives everything from his grace. Here there is no question of becoming autonomous. That would mean aiming to do without God: "I'm strong enough, I have enough experience."

We should beware of a form of desire for perfection that we may sometimes nurture. The desire for perfection

---

10. ms C, 22 rᵒ.

is a good thing in itself, but it can be ambiguous. What do we really want? We would like to be experienced, irreproachable, never make any mistakes, never fall, possess unfailing good judgment and unimpeachable virtue. Which is to say we would like to have no more need of forgiveness or mercy, no more need of God and his help. If at bottom our dream of perfection is to be able to manage without God, we are no longer on the path of the Gospel.

The Gospel path is just the opposite. It leads us to receive everything from God: the meaning of our lives, the courage we need, the light by which we make our choices. It leads us to receive everything from God in trust, prayer and simplicity. That is one aspect of what Thérèse means by "staying little": consenting to receive everything necessary from God's hand, day by day, without worrying about either the past or the future. Day by day, we do what is asked of us, without anxiety, without fear, certain that God is faithful and will give us what we need from moment to moment; never falling prey to the illusion that one day we will be able to manage without God.

Thérèse continued:

> "So I have always stayed little, having no other occupation than that of picking flowers, the flowers of love and sacrifice, and offering them to God for his pleasure."

This means: I don't aim at any extraordinary feats or grandiose deeds that everyone would admire. In the banality of my daily life, I seek to please God in little things, alert for every opportunity of showing simple signs of love, offering myself, etc.—not to accumulate merits or rise above other people, but for love, to please God, as a child seeks to please her father.

> "Being little means not attributing to ourselves the virtues we practice, or believing ourselves capable of anything, but recognizing that God places this treasure in the hands of his little child so that she can use it when she needs it; but the treasure is still God's."

In other words, I practice virtue courageously, but I recognize it is a gift God gives me, so I don't glorify myself for it. All the good I accomplish—and I really try—I attribute to God's goodness. Thérèse was very courageous in practicing all the virtues required by her vocation, but in a balanced way: when she didn't manage as perfectly as she would have wished, she didn't get depressed about it, but accepted the fact that she was sometimes poor and sinful; and when she did manage, it didn't go to her head—she didn't consider herself better than others because of it, but thanked God for the gift he'd given her.

The final sentence is also very important for explaining what "being little" means:

"It means not being discouraged by our faults, because children often fall over, but they are so little they don't hurt themselves badly."

Thérèse was never discouraged by her faults, even when they were sometimes humiliating and painful. There is a great deal of wisdom in what she shares with us: children often fall over and aren't really hurt because they don't fall from a great height (the height of pride, self-sufficiency, etc.) and, what's more, they get right up to throw themselves into their parents' arms and start off again.

These, then, are the main aspects of what St. Thérèse calls "being little." They are what some passages of the Gospel call "becoming like little children"—ultimately, the same as what the Beatitudes in St. Matthew's Gospel mean by being poor in spirit: "Blessed are the poor in spirit, for theirs is the Kingdom of Heaven."[11]

Now lets look more deeply at five of these points: humility, trust, living in the present moment, love, and gratitude. These are, to repeat, fundamental inner attitudes that attract unfailingly God's grace. We must practice them faithfully, do the work that falls to us, and after that keep quiet, so to speak; the rest (our growth in holiness) will happen by itself, God doing his work in us.

---

11. Matthew 5:3.

Let's begin with the two most important, which are the basis for all genuine Christian life: humility and trust. They are inseparable.

What is humility? It seems to me that it has two interconnected aspects.

I've already spoken about the first. Being humble means recognizing everything good and beautiful in my life (my qualities, the good I can do, and so on), as a gift from God. There is more to life than negative things; sometimes we are happy with ourselves, with what we experience and have been able to achieve, and this is justifiable, provided we recognize God as the ultimate source of all those good things. But although we are satisfied and thank our Lord for it, we don't get puffed up by it or consider ourselves better than others because of it. Often enough, however, going beyond the healthy attitude of rejoicing in God for the good we are capable of, we make this a kind of pedestal on which we stand so as to give ourselves the authority to judge other people. That attitude is described in St. Luke's Gospel in the parable of the Publican and the Pharisee:

> God, I thank you that I am not like . . . this tax collector. I fast twice a week, I give tithes of all that I get.[12]

When what is good in our lives becomes a motive for judging and despising others, it's a sign of pride. It comes

---

12. Luke 18:9–14.

(or returns) very quickly, and we need to be on our guard. The right attitude is to rejoice at the good in one's life, while being vigilant to ensure that it doesn't nurture pride, consciously or subconsciously. The two main signs of pride are despising others and getting discouraged.[13] Those who are humble and accept their littleness don't get discouraged because they put their trust in God and not in themselves.

Here we touch on a second absolutely fundamental aspect of humility that is perhaps the most difficult to put into practice.

People sometimes have a false idea of humility. Real humility isn't condemning or despising ourselves, saying scornfully to ourselves, "You're worthless, you're useless." Just the opposite: it is accepting ourselves peacefully as we are—our littleness, physical limitations, psychological weaknesses, lack of courage or virtue, the difficulty we have in praying, all the wretchedness present in our lives, whether physical, mental, or even spiritual. Being humble means consenting to our inner poverty. First of all, recognizing it, because sometimes we don't want to face it, but above all accepting it!

With a bit of clear thinking, we can manage more or less to see our inner poverty. But accepting it is more difficult. We would all like to be more intelligent than we are, stronger, better-looking, more virtuous, more spiritual,

---

13. Proverbs 20.

more this, more that, in any and every sphere of our lives. We can easily get discouraged by the way we are.

Now, very often what prevents God's grace from acting in depth in our lives, and is therefore a kind of sin, is this failure or refusal to accept ourselves as we are: our past, our mistakes, our physique, what we are on the human level, our psychological make-up, our weaknesses, and all the rest.

It isn't easy. I do a lot of listening and spiritual accompanying, and I have heard hundreds of people say, "Father, I just can't accept myself, I can't bear the way I am." Often I have even heard: "I hate myself!"

This is the opposite of humility, of spiritual childhood. Being a child means accepting ourselves as we are. We know we have plenty of limitations and imperfections, but we don't make a production of it and we don't turn it into a major problem. First, we know that God loves us as we are. He doesn't love us for our achievements and successes, but because he has chosen to adopt us, each of us, as his children, and that's that. His love is unconditional. Second, we are sure that out of our weaknesses, our limitations, and even our sins, God, in his astonishing wisdom, can draw some good. We believe in this truth experienced by St. Paul: the power of God is shown forth in human weakness.[14] We don't get upset about our weaknesses, but

---

14. Cf. 2 Corinthians 12:7–10.

accept them in all simplicity. That attitude is an extremely powerful way of attracting God's grace.

Let's consider St. Paul. He was unquestionably endowed with many qualities, but he also had a weak point, a flaw, a "thorn in his flesh." We don't know exactly what it was—it's a disputed question among the scholars. Was it a matter of persistent temptations, a human weakness, some kind of invincible timidity,[15] a sickness? Was it the failure of his apostolate to Jews? For as the Acts of the Apostles bears witness, Paul's apostolate with the Jews was as catastrophic as his apostolate with the Gentiles was fruitful. So we don't know for sure what this flaw was—which is a good thing, since we are left free to apply the concept to all sorts of situations.

Paul bore a burden of suffering and weakness, which was humiliating for him, as he shows by how he describes it: "a messenger of Satan, to harass me, to keep me from being too elated." Or, as we'd say today, he took a beating! Three times Paul begged God to be rid of it, set free from this weakness. And God told him no: "My grace is sufficient for you," you needn't be perfect in every respect. On the contrary, it's good for you to have some points of inner poverty, it protects you, keeps you humble and little, and "my power is made perfect in weakness."[16]

---

15. Cf. 1 Corinthians 2:3: "I was with you in weakness, and much fear and trembling."
16. 2 Corinthians: 7–10.

Paul had to accept that. I don't know how long his trial lasted; it doesn't really matter whether it was a temporary thing or he endured it till the end of his days. There are weaknesses God frees us from, but others he leaves with us, precisely so that we stay small and poor, dependent on his grace, compelled to keep calling out to him all the time. Blessed weaknesses that impel us to call on God! For God hears the prayer of the poor and comes to help them. Sometimes he heals our weaknesses, but sometimes he gives us the grace to live with them trustingly, to accept them peacefully, and accept ourselves as weak and limited.

That is real humility: to accept ourselves as we are, to love ourselves as we are. And it attracts God's grace very powerfully.

3.

BEING RECONCILED
TO OUR WEAKNESS

In learning from Thérèse of Lisieux, we are looking for attitudes that will move God to help us, to grant us the grace we need to progress little by little toward holiness, toward the fullness of love.

In line with the Gospel notion of childhood, these attitudes, which she groups together under the name "littleness," include two basic elements: humility and trust.

We began to look more deeply into humility in the previous chapter. I think a good definition of humility may be this: being in the right relation to ourselves, which enables us to be in the right relation to God and to other people; relating to ourselves according to the truth of what and how we are. One of its essential aspects, as we have seen, is peacefully accepting our weakness and inner poverty.

If we accept ourselves as we are, we also accept God's love for us. But if we reject ourselves, if we despise ourselves, we shut ourselves off from the love God has for us, we deny that love.

If we accept ourselves in our weakness, our limitations, it will also be easier for us to accept other people. Often, quite simply, we can't get along with other people because we can't get along with ourselves. We have all experienced this at some point. Sometimes we are unhappy with ourselves because we've made mistakes or fallen into a fault that humiliates us, so we are really annoyed with ourselves. That makes us bad-tempered and even aggressive with others. What does this mean? Just that we make others pay for our difficulty in accepting our own inner poverty. Not accepting our limitations, we take it out on other people . . . This reaction is very common, and obviously unfair and contrary to the truth. Most of our conflicts others are nothing more than a projection of the conflicts we are having with ourselves.

The opposite is also true. The more we accept ourselves as we are and are reconciled to our own weakness, the more we can accept other people and love them as they are.

But this is sensitive territory. Where do we draw the line between accepting our weakness and complacency about our sins? Sometimes it is not easy to tell the difference. We need to accept our weakness, but clearly we need to reject sin. In the spiritual life we need to find a balance, and it is a subtle one.

On the one hand, we must have a real desire for conversion, a true desire to change, to improve, to live more fully by the Gospel, to practice all the virtues courageously—patience, purity, etc. We must be completely determined about this. It is indispensable to real progress to resolve firmly not to deny God anything.

Take the example of St. Louis, king of France. He told one of his knights, Sire de Joinville, "I would rather catch leprosy than commit a single mortal sin!" In the Middle Ages, that was not to be said lightly, since leprosy meant being cut off from all social contact. And we should be driven by the same determination, preferring to have a painful sickness, or even to die, rather than offend God gravely. We must want to be faithful to God at any cost, ready to "struggle against sin to the point of shedding our blood," as the Letter to the Hebrews says, referring to the possibility of martyrdom.[1] In his famous Rule, St. Benedict likewise exhorts the monks to "prefer nothing to the Love of Christ."

At the same time, though, we need to accept ourselves as interiorly poor and as sinners. Despite our good will and our sincere desire never to refuse God anything and love him with all our hearts, we will come face-to-face with limitations, weaknesses, sometimes falls, that may be very humiliating and that we must

---

1. Cf. Hebrews 12:4.

accept. We need to reject sin yet accept the fact of being poor sinners, people capable of falling often who nevertheless get up again at once, like the little children St. Thérèse speaks of.

So it's a question of finding a balance, and that is delicate but possible. The balance is clearly visible in Thérèse's life: she shows, on the one hand, great courage, great determination to love, to give her life to the end (she was also very demanding of her novices). But on the other hand, little by little, she learned peaceful acceptance of her limitations. Some months before the end of her life, she wrote:

> I am no longer surprised by anything, I am not sorry to see that I am weakness itself. On the contrary, I glory in it, and I expect to discover new imperfections in myself every day.[2]

And again:

> Oh how happy I am to see myself as imperfect and so much in need of God's mercy at the moment of death![3]

Perhaps, too, she expressed herself in these terms because in sickness we can see our poverty more clearly. She accepted it, because she put all her trust in God.

---

2. ms C, 15 r°.
3. YN, July 29, 1897.

We need, then, to practice that same gentleness toward ourselves, that same trust in the mercy of God our Father, and, at the same time, that same determination to belong totally to him, remembering that we cannot serve God and the world, God and money, God and the desire for social success or an easy life at any price. We need to practice gentleness toward ourselves so as not to get discouraged and condemn ourselves when faced with our weakness while also nurturing a great desire for holiness. But not a desire for extraordinary perfection. Holiness is different; it is a real desire to love God and our neighbor and, eschewing a kind of halfway love, go to love's extremes. Thérèse used to say, "I don't want to be half a saint."[4] You can't love God with only 50 percent of your heart. "You shall love the Lord your God with all your heart, and with all your soul, and with all your mind, and you shall love your neighbor as yourself."[5] That is what we should aspire to, not placing our trust in ourselves but relying on God's grace.

To meditate on these matters is also an opportunity for us to stand in the truth about ourselves before God. Sometimes we are a little scared of the truth, but only truth can make us free. Thérèse traveled so quickly toward holiness, I think, because she had a great desire for

---

4. ms A, 10 vº.
5. Matthew 22:37.

the truth. "All I have ever sought is the truth,"[6] she said. She was incapable of lying to herself. And we? We should ask ourselves this question in all sincerity: "What is the deepest desire of my heart?"

We are all men and women of desires. That's normal, the way we are made. We desire many things: happiness, love, life, freedom, and so on. Sometimes our desires are contradictory, and we are divided interiorly, but God wants to bring about the unity of our lives. That is done when from among all our different desires there emerges one aspiration deeper and more essential than the rest. When we examine our consciences lucidly, we know what we want most.

What do we truly aspire to? To love God and neighbor, to live the Gospel message fully? Or less important things that can't really make us happy? I don't say this to arouse fear or guilt, but to point the way to the truth that liberates us. If our deepest desire is to love God and make him loved (the answer Thérèse would have given unhesitatingly had she been asked, "What is your greatest desire?"), we're in good spiritual health. Different people may express it differently, but it makes no difference whether you say your desire is to live the Gospel message, journey toward holiness, reach the fullness of love, respond totally to God's will, or please him in everything.

---

6. YN, September 30, 1897, the day she died.

If that's really our deepest desire (however expressed), God will be truly present in our lives and we will be able to rely on his grace. He will be with us in all things. Nothing will ever be able to separate us from him.

I am describing what is called "good will." We are far from perfect; we commit faults every day without wanting to; but if we are sincere with ourselves, we know that what matters most to us is to live by the Gospel, to answer Jesus' call. Admittedly, many things in life matter to us: our jobs, our families, friends, leisure, holidays, etc. We shouldn't despise such things, because they're good, but from time to time we should check to make sure that our lives are unified by one underlying desire, that of responding to God's call, doing the will of our Father in heaven. That is also our happiness, because what God wants is our happiness. But only he knows the way to it.

Which of us really knows what will make us happy? We want heaps of things. "I'll be happy when I see all my daughters married," "when I've got my degree," "when I've moved to a new apartment," "when I've lost twenty pounds." These are things we can legitimately desire. But let's not lose sight of what is essential. The only thing that can make us absolutely happy is answering God's call to love him and love our neighbor.

We have the right to be poor and little. God isn't shocked by our weaknesses, but he does have a right to find in us the good will described above. To repeat what was said in the previous chapter: Our good will, our sincere desire to do God's will, attracts many graces into our lives. A father can't resist his children's good will. If a father sees his small children, full of good will, trying to solve a problem or face up to a difficulty but having trouble managing by themselves, he will come quickly to help them.

Let's ask the Holy Spirit to help us to harmonize a real desire for holiness, the firm determination to experience ongoing conversion with humility, and the peaceful acceptance of our limitations and weaknesses.

There are situations in life that are not easily judged. I think, for example, of the situations of addiction so frequent today: addictions to alcohol, food, gambling, or sometimes pornography. How much is sin and how much weakness isn't always easy to tell. There is sin where there is freedom—when someone commits a wrong act that could have been avoided. There is sin, too, if one has a weakness, a defect, and does nothing to free himself from it. If we have bad habits we can't break, we need to seek help and talk about it to someone, at least in spiritual guidance. We should seek remedies, sometimes through psychological treatment, as in the case of addictions.

But there are also people who are full of good will, who make an effort, do everything to get help and use it, yet despite all that, can't manage completely to overcome certain problematic weaknesses. They cannot be blamed for that, because they are doing their best, and perhaps it will take them a long time to arrive at real freedom. Such people need to be invited to have patience, accept their inner poverty, place all their hope in God's infinite mercy, and trust that God can draw good out of everything, even the "dark areas" in their lives.

These situations can be complex. Here I can only offer a few guidelines for finding the necessary balance between real desire to progress in holiness and patience toward ourselves, based on trust in God's mercy. Sometimes we're too lazy and don't struggle hard enough against our defects. But sometimes we may fall into the opposite excess: faced with a particular defect that weighs on us, we fight it tooth and nail, insist on wanting to be absolutely rid of it, while God asks us to focus our efforts elsewhere and turn over this defect to him, to sort out in his own good time. If we're in doubt about the right approach, it's good to talk it over with someone else, to have recourse to spiritual guidance. I know that, unfortunately, it isn't always easy to find, but it's always very valuable when we can open our hearts to someone.

Faced with our human weaknesses, we must have a desire for progress and healing, a desire to be formed by the Gospel and the teaching of the Church. But we shouldn't fall into a kind of stubborn "therapeutic obstinacy," with the aim of ridding ourselves absolutely of all imperfections or healing every wound. In doing that, we'd risk becoming impatient and concentrating our efforts on something God isn't specifically asking of us or, ultimately, paying more attention to ourselves than to him.

Before moving on to the theme of trust, let me conclude this point by quoting from one of Thérèse's letters.

Letter no. 197 is addressed to her sister Marie of the Sacred Heart, the second of the Martin daughters to enter Carmel (though she was the eldest). She was Thérèse's godmother. She played a providential role for us, since it was she who suggested to Mother Agnes (Pauline Martin), Mother Superior at the time, to ask Thérèse to write down the childhood memories and other reflections that formed the basis of *The Story of a Soul*. It was not on her personal initiative but in obedience to her superiors that Thérèse started writing. It is fortunate that she obeyed, because the book was an immense gift to the Church.

Among the three autobiographical manuscripts, the shortest, Manuscript B, is in fact a letter addressed to Sister Marie of the Sacred Heart, who had asked Thérèse to share the thoughts in her soul during a retreat she made in September 1896.

This text, just fifteen pages long, is extremely beautiful. In it Thérèse explains that although she knew her vocation (she was a Carmelite, bride of Jesus, and so mother of souls), and was very happy in it, nevertheless she had a certain sense of dissatisfaction. So ardent were her desires to love our Lord and serve the Church that she would have liked to have all the vocations there are—just one wasn't enough for her! She would have liked to be a priest to celebrate Mass with love, a preacher throughout the whole world, a missionary, and even a Papal Zouave[7] to defend the Pope! Above all, she wanted to be a martyr, as the loveliest and highest way to express her love for Jesus. And, not content with just one form of martyrdom, she wanted to undergo all possible kinds!

She knew perfectly well that these desires were excessive, and, as usual, she turned to Scripture in search of a solution. How to live out all the different vocations at once? That seemed mere folly. Then she came upon the words of St. Paul in the First Letter to the Corinthians, saying that even the most perfect gifts are nothing without love. "If I have not love, I am nothing."[8] St. Paul puts it very forcefully: I may speak all the languages of men and angels, possess the fullness of knowledge, strip myself of all my possessions and so on, but without love, without charity, I am nothing at all!

Thérèse sets out a wonderful vision of the mystery of the Church that foreshadows the work of the Second Vatican Council. Her conclusion is that, in the mystical body of the Church, love lies at the basis of all vocations, the love that the Holy Spirit kindles in the hearts of Christians. If this burning love died out, there would be no more missionaries, no more preachers, no more

---

7. The Papal Zouaves were an infantry force formed to defend the Papal States.

8. Cf. 1 Corinthians 13:1–3.

martyrs. . . . There would be nothing at all left in the Church. Love alone is the life of the whole body of the Church; and if I myself make every effort to love in my poor Carmelite convent at Lisieux, in this little corner of Normandy, if I do all I can to love and do everything for love, I am, in a way, living out all the vocations. Love contains all vocations. Then she says something very beautiful:

> I have found my vocation at last: in the heart of my mother the Church I will be Love . . . like that I will be everything . . . and so my dream will be fulfilled![9]

I can't do great things, I can't go off and evangelize, I have no special gifts, but I will be love! And with that I fulfill everything that is indispensable for the Church.

This is very encouraging for us. When we are sick or old, when we feel we haven't much in the way of abilities or talents to put at the service of the Church and are tempted to feel useless, we should remember that the only thing indispensable for the Church is love. Degrees and diplomas, skills, and activities are all admittedly useful, but it is love that counts. Thérèse referred to St. John of the Cross, who said:

> The smallest movement of pure love is more useful to the Church than all other works put together.[10]

---

9. ms B, 3 v°.

10. *Spiritual Canticle*, strophe 29.

Whatever our personal limitations and situations, we can all love right where we are: in the kitchen, the bathroom, the office—it makes no difference. What the Church needs most is genuine love. We attach too much importance to externals, actions, and visible effectiveness, whereas all that counts, all that really bears fruit in the Church, is the truth and purity and sincerity of love; that is what we should ask God for most of all and put into practice.

The sister of the future saint read these beautiful words. She wrote a note to Thérèse (in a Carmelite convent they live mainly in silence and communicate mostly in writing). She told her sister basically this: Your text is magnificent, but it left me with a certain sadness. You ardently desire martyrdom, but I have to admit that what you desire is something I'm scared of! "I flee from what you love," she said. As a result, I am seriously afraid I will never succeed in loving Jesus as much as you do, and that makes me somewhat sad. You have burning, ardent desires, but I am very far from experiencing the same thing in my heart.

Thérèse replied to this little note immediately,[11] not wanting her sister to be left in sadness or discouragement. Her answer is enormously important. I won't quote the whole letter but just a few passages.

---

11. LT 197.

> My darling sister, I don't find it hard to answer you.
> How can you ask if it's possible for you to love God as
> much as I love him? If you had understood the story of
> my little bird, you wouldn't ask that question.

She was speaking of an image she'd used in her first
letter, Manuscript B, comparing herself to a fragile little
bird, incapable of flying like an eagle, that places all its
hope in Jesus, the divine Eagle, who one day will give it
his own wings.

She told her sister it wasn't her burning desires or
any fervor she felt that mattered. Of course, one desire is
necessary. I spoke of it earlier: good will. Other desires
may be marvelous and very strong, especially the kind
to which Thérèse bore witness in saying she wanted to
live out all vocations at the same time and longed to be
a martyr. But she put these desires in their true perspective by saying:

> My desires of martyrdom are nothing, it is not they that
> give me the boundless trust I feel in my heart.

She also added that desires like these can sometimes
be spiritual "riches" in the wrong sense. They make us
unjust "when we repose in them with complacency and
believe that they are something great." Experiencing feelings of strong spiritual fervor, we may sometimes judge
others and judge ourselves more advanced than they.

She explained that these desires were in fact a consolation God gave her because she was weak. She needed encouragement from time to time, and so God made her experience ardent desires on the emotional level. She went on:

> Oh, I am quite sure it is not at all that which pleases God in my little soul.

So that burning fervor was not what pleased God? What did then?

> What pleases him is <u>to see that I love my littleness and my poverty</u>, it is the <u>blind hope that I have in his mercy</u>. . . . That is my only treasure. Darling godmother, why should that treasure not be yours?

These few words are very important. Thérèse underlined them because they put things in the right perspective. She did not deny all she had lived and explained, her times of grace and fervor, but she was fully aware that these were not what made her pleasing to God. What pleased God in her was, rather, her love for her own littleness and inner poverty, and her blind hope in God's mercy. Humility and trust. This is what unfailingly makes us pleasing to God, draws down his grace upon our souls, and makes us the object of his tenderness and love. "That is my only treasure," she told her sister.

And it can also perfectly well be yours. Maybe you don't always feel great desires, an impetuous longing for martyrdom. But loving your littleness and placing absolute trust in God is always within your reach! You can do that without any difficulty.

A little further on, Thérèse added three further helpful considerations.

> We must consent to stay poor and feeble, and that is what is so difficult. For "where is the truly poor in spirit to be found? He is to be sought very far off," as the psalmist said. . . . He did not say one must seek him among the great souls, but "very far," that is, in lowness, in nothingness. . . . Oh, let us keep away, then, from everything that shines; let us love our littleness, let us love not feeling anything, then we will be poor in spirit and Jesus will come to find us however far away we are, and will transform us into flames of love.

These lines convey a magnificent hope: if we accept our littleness without ever becoming discouraged, then our Lord in person will come running to find us, and will transform us into a flame of love. It is he who will make our hearts burn with love and charity—however far away we are, however poor we are, however low we have perhaps fallen.

Thérèse continues:

Oh, how I would like to be able to make you understand what I feel! . . . It is trust and nothing but trust that must lead us to Love.

Hers is a path of littleness but, still more fundamentally, a path of trust. That is the most characteristic feature of spiritual childhood.

A very small child never doubts his father's love but trusts him absolutely. Small children are astonishing in this trust of theirs. A father can stand his small son on a table, move back, and tell the little boy, "Jump!" and the child will jump. He won't stop to wonder whether his father will catch him or let him fall. Such thoughts don't trouble him for an instant.

This unlimited trust in God's goodness and faithfulness lies at the heart of the path to holiness.

Conversely, in one of her letters Thérèse says that what hurts God most, our most serious failings in this regard, is our lack of trust. "What offends Jesus, what wounds his heart, is lack of trust."[12] God does not first expect of us that we be absolutely perfect (that will come little by little) but that we give him our trust—trust that has to be total.

I know that this isn't so easy to do, since we are all somewhat wounded when it comes to trust. This is a remnant

---

12. Letter 192 to her cousin Marie Guérin, who was blaming herself for temptations against purity, and had stopped receiving Holy Communion for this reason.

left of original sin: man distrusts God, is scared of God, runs away from God instead of trusting him completely.

Thérèse fully understood how trust draws God's grace down on our lives. If we have an attitude of trust, we can be certain we are open to God's love. We also need the good will I spoke of earlier, as well as humility, of course, but trust has a special power. Thérèse loved this quotation from St. John of the Cross: "One obtains from God as much as one hopes for."[13] "Be it done for you as you have believed," Jesus says in the Gospel.[14]

This trust is not easy to practice. We all have fears, worries, doubts, and suspicions, areas where we remain resolutely closed. The devil always tries to make us doubt God's love. Not only does he accuse men before God, he also accuses God to men. We see this clearly in the Book of Genesis.[15] When God forbids Adam to eat of the tree of the knowledge of good and evil, the devil raises suspicion about God, accusing him of having ulterior motives, refusing to let man have something that would be good for him.

The devil always seeks to make us doubt God's love. By contrast, the Holy Spirit will always encourage and help us to trust God. This is one of the fundamental points of the little way. Among the graces we can obtain

---

13. *The Dark Night of the Soul,* Book II, Chapter 21.
14. Cf. Matthew 9:29.
15. Cf. Genesis 3:4–5.

from St. Thérèse, let's ask her for greater trust in our Lord, in his faithfulness and goodness.

Even if you have suffered, even if you have sometimes been disappointed by life, even if, at certain times, you had the feeling that God was very far away (we all have this feeling when living through a time of trial) or had abandoned you, in spite of all of that, never doubt God's love, never doubt his faithfulness.

Give him, or restore to him, today, *all* your trust, like a little child giving all his trust to his loving father. Not 50 percent, not even 95 percent, but 100 percent.

God deserves our total trust, because he is our Father. True, God's wisdom is mysterious, it isn't always our kind of wisdom; in our lives and in the life of the world and the Church, he allows things that to us seem surprising or even scandalous, so that we might want things to be different. That is all part of the battle to be human. But let's never doubt God's love.

The greater our trust is, the more we will experience God's faithfulness and see how true it is that, as Paul told the Romans, everything works together for the good of those who love him.[16]

---

16. Cf. Romans 8:28.

4.

TRUSTING MORE AND MORE

We asked ourselves the question "What does 'becoming a little child again' mean?" After referring to humility, we spoke of trust, the most fundamental characteristic of the "littleness" of the Gospel.

Thérèse talks about it a lot. Her insistence on the importance of trust is based on her rediscovery of God as Father. At a time when people placed enormous stress on God's severity and justice, when traces of Jansenism were still very evident in Catholic thinking, this rediscovery of the face of God as a merciful Father was badly needed.

Obviously, it's not possible to set God's justice in opposition to his mercy or to get rid of the notion of justice, but Thérèse rediscovered a true understanding of these divine attributes. This is what she said about God's justice in one of her letters,[1] quoting Psalm 103 (8–14):

---

1. LT 226.

I know that the Lord is infinitely just and it is that justice, which terrifies so many souls, that is the reason for my joy and trust. Being just does not only mean exercising severity to punish the guilty, it also means recognizing upright intentions and rewarding virtue. I hope for as much from God's justice as from his mercy. It is because he is just that "he is merciful and gracious, slow to anger and abounding in steadfast love . . . for he knows our weakness, he remembers that we are dust. . . . As a father pities his children, so the Lord pities us."

God is not scandalized by our weaknesses. Provided he finds in us good will and trust, we can be certain of pleasing him.

Many passages very beautifully illustrate how Thérèse saw God as Father—"It is so sweet to call God our Father!"[2]—and what a great light this was for her whole life.

This rediscovery was greatly facilitated by her experience of family life. Her own father was an exceptional man, with whom she had a wonderful father-daughter relationship. Not all of us are lucky enough to have a father like Louis Martin. We may have had very difficult relationships with our fathers involving indifference,

---

2. Conversation recorded by her sister Céline. *A Memoir of My Sister St. Thérèse*, 1959, p. 109.

neglect, or excessive harshness. And it must be said that being a father and finding the right way to act in this difficult but marvelous vocation isn't easy. Fathers are often weak, wounded people; as a result, their children are too.

But in our relationship with God—in prayer, in the discovery of his fatherly love—we can little by little find deep healing. I think this privileged access to God as Father is one of the main fruits of prayer, particularly mental prayer, silent prayer.

This filial relationship with God, expressed and deepened especially in prayer, is not always easy to develop today. It is not obvious how to live as little children in such a pitiless, competitive world. We must be adult, able sometimes to fight, while still keeping a child's heart which rests in God and abandons itself to him. He will certainly know how to defend us. He is our Father, and he is faithful. All too often we get agitated instead of relying trustingly on God.

This work of restoring trust in our hearts is an essential aspect of the spiritual life. Wounded by original sin, our hearts are riddled with fears and doubts. It takes time to be cured of them. Maybe that will never happen completely in this life, but we can nevertheless make great strides in trusting more.

With that aim, I want to say some words about how we can grow in this area. Our trust in God is weak and fragile. What specifically can we do to strengthen and increase it?

One very valuable resource, already mentioned, is Sacred Scripture. Multiple passages from the Old and New Testaments invite us to trust:

> The Lord is my light and my salvation: whom shall I fear?[3]

> Fear not, little flock, for it is your Father's good pleasure to give you the kingdom.[4]

> Do not be afraid . . . are not five sparrows sold for two pennies? And not one of them is forgotten before God. Why, even the hairs of your head are all numbered. Fear not; you are of more value than many sparrows![5]

> I am with you always, to the close of the age.[6]

The Bible offers many passages like these to reassure us. In particular, it contains that school of prayer, the Psalms, whose words appeal to all cultures. Whether one is Chinese, African, or Spanish, this is a universal language, simple and specific: the Lord is my rock, my rampart, my refuge, my fortress, etc.

---

3. Psalm 27:1.

4. Luke 12:32.

5. Luke 12:6–7.

6. Matthew 28:20.

For my father and my mother have forsaken me, but the Lord will take me up.[7]

We find the same language in the Prophets, such as Isaiah:

The mountains may depart and the hills be removed, but my steadfast love shall not depart from you.[8]

If we lack trust, it's often because we do not nourish ourselves enough on God's Word. Everyone who has frequent and assiduous recourse to Scripture has had the experience of one day being troubled or discouraged when a verse of Scripture touched her, restored her trust and brought peace to her heart once again. Holy Scripture is one of the richest, most beautiful, and most effective resources at our disposal. It possesses a power and authority no human words can have, and it can do much to nurture our trust in God. (That presupposes, of course, that we persevere in reading and praying about God's Word.)

Another thing that increases our trust is to make acts of faith. Faith grows when it is exercised. What is an act of faith? It's very simple. We are tempted to worry, for instance, because we're going to have major surgery in two weeks, or one of our children is going through a difficult time. We say to our Lord, "I trust you. I leave this situation

---

7. Psalm 27:10.
8. Isaiah 54:10.

in your hands, and I know you'll look after it." There are thousands of examples like that. I am a great believer in the effectiveness of acts of faith.

We're not talking here about a magic wand that makes every problem disappear. But those little choices of trust and faith will bear fruit sooner or later. It may be only in ten or twenty years' time; that doesn't matter. I love the Gospel image of the grain of mustard seed. It is the smallest of all seeds, but when sown in the ground it grows up into almost a tree. All those acts of faith that may seem sterile, with no immediate results that we can see, are like seeds. Those seeds will unfailingly bear fruit in due course. It doesn't matter whether in five minutes or ten years: let's allow God's wisdom to work.

Making those acts of trust does not make difficulties vanish, but it causes us to experience God's faithfulness in reply. "Trust works miracles," says St. Thérèse.[9] Not always the way we imagine, sometimes very differently from what we expect, but God always responds to our trust in the end. So making those acts of faith makes us enter more and more deeply into the experience of God's faithfulness. We realize that in this or that situation, which seemed absolutely insoluble, things have mysteriously sorted themselves out. I have a firm belief in this; it is a very simple and unassuming approach to God, but in

---

9. LT 129.

the long term it is very effective. It is faith that saves, says the Bible, and that is a statement of fact—not just words or campaign promises.

Another thing that nourishes trust (I referred to it briefly earlier) is discovering the true face of God. Not the God we imagine, the product of our human, psychological ideas, but the living and true God. In the Book of Job we find this phrase: "I had heard of thee by the hearing of the ear, but now my eye sees thee!"[10] We can all see God, discover God's true face. Not necessarily in ecstasies and visions (I've never had any of those!) but by growing in faith. True, Scripture says no one can see God; we shall only see him face-to-face in the next life. Here below, however, we can have a real experience of God and can come to know him. In the Old Testament—the Book of Jeremiah, chapter 31, verses 33–34—we find a magnificent passage that speaks of the New Covenant that will come about with the gift of the Spirit:

> But this is the covenant which I will make with the house of Israel after those days, says the Lord: I will put my law within them, and I will write it upon their hearts; and I will be their God, and they shall be my people. And no longer shall each man teach his neighbor

10. Job 42:5.

and each his brother, saying, "Know the Lord," for they shall all know me, from the least of them to the greatest, says the Lord; for I will forgive their iniquity, and I will remember their sin no more.

This passage announces that everyone is offered a very deep knowledge of God, closely linked to the revelation of his mercy. The deepest knowledge of God available to us in this life passes through the experience of divine mercy, God's forgiveness. This promise of Scripture is for us, especially in the present time. For in today's world, if you can't see God, if you don't know God, there is a great danger of becoming disoriented and totally lost.

Happily, God himself assures us: "They shall all know me, from the least to the greatest." We could even say, "especially the least of them!" St. Luke's Gospel tells us Jesus exulted for joy in the Holy Spirit, and said:

I thank thee, Father, Lord of heaven and earth, that thou hast hidden these things from the wise and understanding and revealed them to babes; yea, Father, for such was thy gracious will. All things have been delivered to me by my Father; and no one knows who the Son is except the Father, or who the Father is except the Son and any one to whom the Son chooses to reveal him.[11]

---

11. Luke 10:21–22.

The revelation of the Father comes through the Son. God wants to show his face to men. And men have deformed it so badly, have accused God so terribly! This is the drama of atheism: God has been thrown into the rubbish bin, accused of being man's enemy, an obstacle to our freedom, a God who crushes us, etc.

Today more than ever, God wants to reveal himself to our hearts, simply, gently, in the darkness of faith, but in a very profound way, so that each of us can achieve a real knowledge of his being. In the sixteenth century, St. John of the Cross said:

> The Lord has always revealed the treasures of his wisdom and his spirit to mortals, but now that evil is showing its face more, God reveals them to us still more fully.[12]

What would he say if he were alive today! I'm convinced that God wants to reveal himself more than ever to all the little children, the poor, who we are.

One of the paths of this revelation, a secret but privileged one, is the mystery of the Blessed Virgin Mary. It is wonderful to see how Mary is present today in the life of the world. If we entrust ourselves to her, if we let ourselves be taught by her, she gives us access to a true knowledge of God, because she introduces us into the depths of prayer.

---

12. Maxim 6 in the collection given to Mother Francisca of the Mother of God.

That is where God reveals himself and shows us his face. Recently I was talking to a group about the experience of certain people to whom Mary appears regularly today and whom she is teaching personally. The response was, "They're so lucky!" So they are; but in fact our Lady does the same for everyone who asks it of her, but she does it invisibly. If we believe her and place ourselves entirely in her hands, she forms and teaches us and grants us a real knowledge of God.

Little Thérèse would not have become what she was without the deep devotion to Mary that surrounded her as she was growing up. Clearly she is a soul formed by Mary.[13]

There is a passage in *The Secret of Mary* by St. Louis-Marie Grignion de Montfort (whose teaching on Mary, as we know, was of great significance to Blessed John Paul II) that says God is present everywhere, we can find him everywhere, but in Mary he makes himself present to little children and the poor in a very particular way.

> Nowhere is God more present to us and more sympathetic to human weakness than in Mary. It was for this very purpose that he came down from heaven. Everywhere else he is the Bread of the strong and the Bread of Angels, but in Mary he is the Bread of children. [14]

---

13. Littleness is a grace from Mary. One verse of Thérèse's beautiful poem about our Lady says: "In your sight, O Mary, I love to be a child." PN 54.

14. The Secret of Mary, First Part, no. 20.

In Mary, God becomes food for little children. In her, we find God in his greatness and majesty, his power and wisdom, all that completely surpasses us, yet at the same time an accessible God who doesn't overwhelm, doesn't destroy, but gives himself to be our life.

On May 13, 2000, when two of the little shepherd children of Fatima, Francisco and Jacinta, were beatified, Pope John Paul II gave a beautiful homily. You can find it easily on the Vatican website.

The Pope talked about the Gospel passage I referred to earlier: what God has hidden from the wise and prudent, he has revealed to little children. The Holy Father spoke of one of the experiences the ones at Fatima had when our Lady appeared to them:

> And behold, they see a light shining from her maternal hands which penetrates them inwardly, so that they feel immersed in God just as—they explain—a person sees himself in a mirror.

When Francisco talked about this experience afterwards, he said:

> We were burning in that light which is God and we were not consumed. What is God like? It is impossible to say. In fact we will never be able to tell people.

They were plunged in the fire of God's love, not a fire that destroys but one that lights and warms, a fire full of ardor and life. The Pope linked this to the Old Testament and Moses' experience at the burning bush.

> Moses had the same experience when he saw God in the burning bush; he heard God say that he was concerned about the slavery of his people and had decided to deliver them through him: "I will be with you."[15] Those who welcome this presence become the dwelling-place and, consequently, a "burning bush" of the Most High.

It is very touching to see how those young children of Fatima, ignorant in so many ways, experienced something very similar to what a great Old Testament figure like Moses experienced. When our Lady asked them to pray for Russia, they thought at first that "Russia" was a sinful woman for whom they should intercede! Through Mary, these simple children entered into a very profound experience of the living God.

We needn't envy them. We won't have the same direct experience they did, but on the level of faith we can all have access to the same realities and come to know God, the littlest of us as much as the greatest, and so become "burning bushes of the Most High." This is the promise contained in Scripture:

---

15. Cf. Exodus 3:2–12.

It shall come to pass afterward, that I will pour out my spirit on all flesh.[16]

The earth shall be full of the knowledge of the Lord as the waters cover the sea.[17]

That is God's promise for the end times. And we are there. . . . Marthe Robin, a great French mystic, announced a Pentecost of love and mercy on the whole world. It has already begun. Of course we should not start speculating about when the world will end; that is always very dangerous. The Church may last a long time yet, but we can feel an undeniable spiritual urgency. The world is suffering at many levels. The economic crises we are currently going through are only one tiny symptom; there are other, much more painful aspects. So many young people are lost, with no meaning for their lives. They follow the vilest and most destructive ways of life and enslave themselves to the stupidest fashions and worst addictions. St. Teresa of Avila said:

The world is burning; now is not the time to be talking of unimportant things.

Faced with all this, however, we should not get anxious. On the contrary, we should be more and more

16. Joel 2:28.
17. Isaiah 11:9.

trusting and childlike and peaceful. Mary is the Queen of Peace, and the more crisis-stricken the world is, the more we must be at peace and receive God's peace, for we can be certain of his love and faithfulness.

While we need to be clear and realistic about the present state of the world, I have no wish at all to use melodramatic terms to stir up fear. Fear is one of our worst enemies. Do not be afraid! Fear not! This is what Jesus tells us constantly. Paul asks, "If God is for us, who is against us?"[18] And God *is* for us: he has shown that by giving us his Son who died for us while we were still sinners, as St. Paul says in the same letter to the Romans.[19] So we should not be anxious, but full of trust and peace. To do so, however, we need to be firmly rooted in God, to live by his love, his word, and let him reveal his face to us as our Father, so that we can enter into the true freedom of God's children.

Our prayer life is of capital importance from this point of view. What the Church needs most is prayer, adoration. I know it isn't always easy, with the pace of life today as it is, but we have to find time for prayer. We have to make time for a heart-to-heart conversation with God. There need to be places with Exposition of the Blessed Sacrament, where we can spend time in adoration. Today,

---

18. Romans 8:31.
19. Cf. Romans 5:8.

thank God, there are churches that have Exposition of the Blessed Sacrament twenty-four hours a day.

God does not ask everyone for the same thing, but everyone does need a minimum of faithfulness in prayer. We should devote more time to prayer, to adoration, when we have the opportunity. That is not a waste of time—just the opposite, it's a breath of fresh air for the world. There is nothing more ecological than prayer!

It's not only nature that needs saving. The main endangered species today is not the polar bear but the human race. Yes, people should try to save the polar bears. They are created by God and beautiful, and the little bear cubs are delightful. But the most important task of all is to save mankind, and mankind will be saved by prayer. The works of apostolate and charity must be the result of prayer and contemplation.

Not everyone can spend hours in church, but each of us must do the little he or she can. If there were a little less television and a little more prayer in our lives, we would be more at peace. For each hour of television news, I think, one needs at least an hour of adoration to be able to digest all that news—not always good news—that floods us.

Let's each of us do what God asks in this. I know it isn't easy. Faithfulness to prayer requires a lot of effort, but it is worthwhile. To be faithful to prayer, you need to establish a rhythm, since our lives are made up of rhythms and we need good habits, including established times when we pray, and that's all there is to it. No questioning it: this is a firm decision we've made. It requires a struggle at the start, but afterwards it brings us great joy.

There's a common difficulty, though. When we regularly spend time in prayer, it goes very well sometimes but not always. A half hour or hour before the Blessed Sacrament may be a time of beauty and gentleness during which we may experience great happiness, a happiness not of this world. But we may also find it tedious and boring, and think the time goes very slowly. Our times of prayer may be times of poverty and distraction; when we are alone in silence before God, all our problems come crowding into our minds! Regrets for the past, fears about the future, all the things that aren't going well, whatever causes us anxiety: all this comes to the surface. It isn't at all pleasant, but we must persevere. And if we do, sooner or later something wonderful will happen.

Prayer follows laws that are flexible and unpredictable, but what I'm going to sketch now remains basically valid. If we are faithful to our times of prayer, little by little we will be given peace. For God is an ocean of peace, and he will grant it to us. God will give us the grace to accept all those defects of which we become aware. Being reconciled with ourselves requires some hard work but that is one of the fruits of prayer.

When a person is faithful to his or her times of prayer, day after day, week after week, it's like someone with a well in the garden that's choked with rubbish—branches, leaves, stones, mud—but underneath is water, clean and pure. In spending time in prayer, you're setting to work patiently to unblock the well. What comes up at the start is the mud and dirt: our wretchedness, worries, fears, guilt, self-blame—the things we normally avoid. Plenty of people run away from themselves. There's a real fear of silence today! But those who have the courage to go forward into the desert end up finding an oasis.

Let's stay with the image of the well. We start digging, and at first it's not very pleasant, because we come face-to-face with our limitations and human deficiencies. But if we persevere, we'll end by finding the wellspring. We discover, to our joy, that at the bottom of our hearts flows a pure spring of water, the presence of God dwelling within us. Even if we are poor sinners, by going to the depths of our hearts in prayer we find pure, clear water. But only prayer grants us access to the bottom of our hearts. Therapy, even psychoanalysis, can only stay on the surface. Sometimes it's necessary; it can be useful in clearing stuff away. But the only things that gives us access to the depths of our hearts, to our deepest identity, to the child of God that each of us is, are faith and prayer.

Faith and prayer enable us to discover the presence of God in us, a pure, ever-flowing spring of water by which we are washed and renewed. We discover the true face of God, God in his fatherhood, his mercy, his absolute and unconditional love. At the same time, we discover our deepest selves. It is through faithfulness to prayer that we enter into a real experience of God and a real knowledge of ourselves. The whole of the Christian life, in all its various aspects and dimensions, is of course involved in this process, with its ups and downs; there's no magic wand. But in the long run, faithfulness to prayer transforms our lives in depth. The members of the Institute of Notre Dame de Vie (Our Lady of Life), who live the Carmelite spirituality, do two hours of prayer every day. In my own Community of the Beatitudes, we do an hour of silent adoration daily. For others it will be a bit less, perhaps only a quarter of an hour, but the same faithfulness is always necessary.

Let me give you my personal testimony. At one stage, when I was twenty-three, my life was going very badly. I was in a state of great confusion. Then I decided to make a one-week spiritual retreat in a Cistercian monastery. I came away with just one idea: that God was asking me to spend a quarter of an hour in prayer every day, but that had to be "sacred" and untouchable. Sometimes I'd come in at two in the morning after being out with friends, and I still did my quarter of an hour's prayer if I hadn't been able to do it earlier. I received the grace of faithfulness; God had pity on me. And I found that, little by little, that time of prayer changed my life. I recovered the peace and trust I'd lost. The quarter-hour slowly grew. I began to spend more time praying, and God led me by means of that regular prayer.

God does not ask us to pray "well," but he does invite us to pray without getting tired of it or becoming discouraged.[20] He asks us for a prayer of faithfulness. We know the emphasis laid by St. Teresa of Avila on the determination to be faithful to personal mental prayer, the "exchange of friendship in which we converse frequently and intimately with the One who we know loves us."[21] She says something very important: people who do mental prayer don't become saints overnight, they fall from time to time, but they will always have the grace to get up again, and from each fall they will spring up higher.[22]

Let's ask for the grace of faithfulness in prayer, for our parish communities or others, and for ourselves personally. Let's pray in particular that there may be more places of adoration in the Church. I am convinced this will transform very many things. All the great spiritual renewals, and even the renewals of society, begin by renewals of prayer. That includes community prayer, liturgical prayer, charismatic prayer, but above all, personal prayer.

If the charismatic renewal movement doesn't culminate in a renewal of mysticism, it is worthless. Mysticism

---

20. Cf. Luke 18:1.

21. *Autobiography*, chapter 8.

22. Cf. *Autobiography*, chapter 19.

does not mean experiencing extraordinary things; it means entering into intimacy with God, a personal experience of God. This experience is very simple, as I said before; it takes place in faith, but it makes us really live by God and let ourselves be led by him. When we consider St. Thérèse of Lisieux's prayer life, we can see that most of the time she was very simple and even interiorly poor. She was unlike St. Teresa of Avila, who had constant visions and ecstasies. On two or three occasions, Thérèse of Lisieux received special graces in prayer, but in general she lived her prayer life in great simplicity and even a certain dryness. It didn't matter. She was there, God was there, and that was enough.

In a beautiful passage, Thérèse sets out her experience in this matter. Usually nothing special happened in her prayer; there were no great lights or sensations. But because she was faithful to it, she received the lights she needed outside her times of prayer:

> I understand and I know from experience that "the kingdom of God is within us." Jesus does not need books or learned doctors to instruct souls. He who is the doctor of doctors teaches without any need of words. . . . I have never heard him speak, but I feel that he is in me, that at every moment he is guiding me, inspiring me with what I should say or do. Just when I need it, I discover lights that I had not seen before. It is

not usually during my prayer that they are most abundant, but rather amidst my daily occupations.[23]

I find this passage tremendously significant. That is often the way things happen in our lives. Apparently nothing in particular happens during the actual time of prayer, but because we have been faithful to it, God instructs us in secret, he places things in us without our being aware of it. And when we need to give someone advice or have to make a decision, we receive a light there and then.

This means that even if our prayer is a bit arid, we must never be discouraged. God deposits treasures secretly in our hearts for the times when we will need them. That's logical. We don't need great lights in prayer, we need them in making decisions and acting. In prayer it is enough for us to stay humbly in God's presence. "He looks at me, and I look at him," a worthy peasant of Ars, who spent some time at the back of the church every day, said when the holy Curé of Ars asked him how he prayed.

Today, I'm sure, God grants many graces of prayer like that, simple but profound, because he wants to reveal himself and renew his people.

May little Thérèse obtain for us the grace of faithfulness to prayer, in accordance with what God wants of

---

23. ms a, 83 v°.

each of us. May each of us be able to understand what is being asked of us, what daily or weekly faithfulness to our meetings with our Lord we need to show today. God is waiting for us: let's not leave him alone!

5.

GOD'S INFINITE MERCY

Someone once asked me how to combine the attitude of littleness to which Thérèse invites us with the need to survive in this world, where any weakness or fragility can quickly put us out of the game.

I think it's not a question of merely surviving; we have to live in this world positively and confidently. And it's never been easy to practice the Gospel in society. Think of the first Christians, immersed in a pagan universe. It can't have been so easy for them.

Jesus speaks in the Gospel about this ongoing tension between Christian values and the values of society.

I send you out as sheep in the midst of wolves. [1]

---

1. Matthew 10:16.

There's realism! But it doesn't mean we're necessarily going to be eaten. God will always be our protection and refuge. In St. John's gospel, Jesus adds:

In the world you have tribulation, but be of good cheer, I have overcome the world.[2]

We shouldn't despise the world as such, but we should be vigilant about what is bad in the spirit of the world. Especially, we need to know that Jesus has overcome it. We should never lose confidence.

The basic command Jesus gives to these sheep he sends out in the midst of wolves is to be "wise as serpents and innocent as doves."[3] We must try to practice both attitudes at once. On the one hand, showing wisdom and intelligence, thinking ahead about what we are saying and to whom, being ready sometimes to defend ourselves (or rather, to defend what is most precious to us), being clear-minded, mature, showing initiative. But on the other hand, we should also keep our hearts pure and childlike. Thérèse says to Jesus in one of her poems:

I want to love you like a little child, I want to battle like a warrior bold.[4]

---

2. John 16:33.
3. Matthew 10:16.
4. PN 36.

We have to fight in this world but keep our hearts pure. It's possible. We can do it by not letting negative reactions take hold of us—fear, worry, defense mechanisms, bitterness, resentment, selfishness, duplicity, politicking, and calculation. How is it possible to prevent them? By practicing Thérèse's message: through simplicity, trusting self-abandonment, humility, faithfulness to prayer. . . . God looks after our hearts when we give them constantly to him. He purifies them, renews them, and fills them with peace.

When Jesus sends his disciples out on their mission, he tells them, "Beware of men,"[5] and at the same time, "So have no fear of them."[6] Be prudent but not fearful. He asks them to go in poverty and precarious living, without taking any money or a spare tunic, but he also says something very powerful that is not sufficiently remarked upon: "Nothing shall hurt you."[7]

Even in a difficult world marked by evil, our hearts can remain pure if they belong to God, if we love God and practice all that we've discussed so far. It is not always easy, but it is possible, and God grants his grace in proportion to the difficulties. When times are harder, graces are more abundant and more powerful. Today, as I said

---

5. Matthew 10:17.
6. Matthew 10:26.
7. Luke 10:19.

before, there are some very powerful graces of knowledge of God and listening to his Word.

We should have very great trust. When going through times of trouble and worry, read Psalm 23.

> The Lord is my shepherd, I shall not want. . . . Even though I walk through the valley of the shadow of death, I fear no evil, for thou art with me.

What helps most to keep our hearts pure are trust and hope.

Now I want to take up the thread of our meditations on Thérèse's spiritual experience and her discovery of the "little way." She wanted to be a saint, to love God with her whole being, to serve the Church and the world, and she felt very small, powerless. So she looked for an elevator to lift her to God—she looked for the attitudes that would enable God's grace to come and take her where she couldn't manage to go by herself.

We have talked about some of these attitudes: humility, accepting our littleness, and trust—"a blind hope in God's mercy," as Thérèse put it in the letter quoted above.[8]

Let's return to the subject of trust. We have seen how we should nurture our trust. It is fragile, but it can be increased and strengthened by listening to the Word, by

---

8. LT 197.

prayer, by the acts of faith we make in difficult moments, and by the experience of God's faithfulness.

Now I wish to make a point that is simple but has wide implications. I can put it in the form of a question: What is the basis for our trust? What does it actually rest on?

It is essential that it be truly trust *in God*. Sometimes we are more or less under an illusion about this. Speaking of her great desires and the fervor she experienced in the letter quoted above, Thérèse said, "It is not they that give me the boundless trust I feel in my heart." She is careful to make it clear that her trust is not based on herself, her desires, her qualities, or her virtues, but only on God.

Sometimes we manage to do what is right, lead a good and virtuous life, have great trust in God, without the slightest problem; and then a difficult time comes. For instance, we commit a fault that really humiliates us. Or we make a wrong decision, which is unpleasant, especially when other people notice it. We are brought face-to-face with our defects, and we become sad and discouraged. All our great trust in God melts away like snow in the sun.

This simply means that what we called trust in God was in fact trust in ourselves. If trust disappears when we do wrong, it shows that our trust was based on ourselves and our deeds. Discouragement is a clear sign that we've put our trust in ourselves and not at all in God.

Trust that is truly based on God, whether we're doing well or badly, whether we're happy or unhappy with ourselves, should never waver. . . . God's love is not subject to eclipses. And it is vital that our trust should rest not on our personal achievements but only on God's love, his tenderness, his infinite mercy, on the fact that he is our Father and can never abandon us. Otherwise we will never be truly free but will always be afraid of failure, of our weaknesses and somewhat centered on ourselves instead of centered on God.

There is a subtle but very common temptation in the spiritual life. With the excuse of wanting to be perfect, we seek to examine our inner selves too much, to evaluate ourselves and measure our progress. The usual result is that a sort of discontent and permanent sadness slips into our lives, since we are never fully satisfied with ourselves. Such an attitude causes us to center on ourselves, when what we need to do is throw ourselves on God with unlimited trust. We're more concerned about ourselves than about God. The only way really to forget ourselves is by placing all our hope in God. I don't mean we shouldn't examine our consciences: that is something we must do. But we should ensure that examination of conscience doesn't degenerate into gazing gloomily at ourselves. The best way to enlighten our consciences and discern our real sins is to look at God, to take his Word as our mirror.[9]

---

9. Cf. St. James, 1:23–24.

Before going on to other subjects, let's look at a passage by Thérèse on the subject of trust. It's from a letter to Fr. Bellière,[10] one of her two "spiritual brothers"—priests for whom she was asked to pray and to whom she wrote some very interesting letters explaining her "little way." This passage shows how she rediscovered God as Father, as well as the extent to which trust makes us pleasing to God and attracts his graces.

> I would like to try and make you understand by a very simple comparison how much Jesus loves souls, including imperfect ones, who entrust themselves to Him. Imagine that a father has two naughty, disobedient sons and when he comes to punish them, he sees one of them running away in fear and trembling, knowing in his heart of hearts that he deserves to be punished . . .

So that is the attitude of the first son. The second is much more crafty—but crafty in the right way, as we shall see!

> . . . while his brother does the opposite: he throws himself into his father's arms, telling him that he is sorry to have hurt him, that he loves him, and that he will prove it by being good from now on.

And that's not all:

10. LT 258.

Then, if that child asks his father to <u>punish</u> him with a <u>kiss</u>,[11] I don't think the happy father could harden his heart against his child's filial trust, knowing his sincerity and love.

Of course, the child's love has to be genuine, with a real desire to behave better. But he also has daring trust.[12]

Of course, he knows that his son will fall into the same faults again and again, but he is ready to forgive him every time, if his son catches him by the heart every time.

We too should "catch God by the heart," drawing down his grace and forgiveness by our trust. God can't hold out against his children's trust in him. It must of course spring from true, sincere love, but we can obtain everything from God through trust, especially the forgiveness and mercy we need so badly, because we are sinners, our hearts are hard, and we don't love enough.

I think this beautiful passage from St. Thérèse could be the basis for a whole course on confession, which is the sacrament of mercy. We have a great need for it, and it's a pity so many Catholics no longer go to confession. They deprive themselves of a very profound experience of God's mercy, of the fatherly tenderness Thérèse tells us about.

---

11. Underlined by Thérèse in the original.

12. Thérèse talks several times about this idea of loving trust that even becomes daring . . . ms C, 36 v°; LT 247.

Confession, when it is done well, properly and with the right attitude, is a privileged means for helping us to rediscover God's real face, his infinite love, his forgiveness, his generosity, and his unbelievable patience toward us.

To make a good confession, we must of course begin by being really repentant, recognizing the sins of which we are guilty, and not making excuses, justifying ourselves, or blaming other people. Instead of finding thousands of extenuating circumstances, we have to say: I have truly sinned, my heart was hard, I was proud, I despised my neighbor, I sought my own pleasure at other people's expense, I forgot about God . . . and so on, stating all the sins we are aware of. Repentance is a necessity: sincere regret for the faults we have committed. It isn't measured so much by our feelings as by our desire to be converted and begin over again. The Desert Fathers said that someone who weeps for his sins is greater than someone who raises the dead! In the Beatitudes,[13] we find this phrase: "Blessed are those who mourn, for they shall be comforted." This can be applied to many kinds of tears, but especially to the tears of repentance.

Jesus tells us that everyone who humbles himself will be exalted. The publican stood far off in the Temple and said, "God, be merciful to me, a sinner!"[14] This man was

13. Matthew 5:3–12.
14. Luke 18:9–14.

justified, saved, healed, and profoundly renewed, because he recognized his sins clearly and sincerely. Real repentance is a huge grace that leads to great happiness, the joy of being purified and set free, of receiving a new heart and new freedom to love.

After repentance comes the petition for forgiveness. Then we receive pardon through the words of the priest. By the way, when we priests say to someone, "I absolve you from your sins!" it's a wonderful moment for us. Faced with someone suffering over his faults, perhaps feeling crushed by the weight of his guilt, it is such a joy to be able to pronounce those liberating words, bringing the grace that really transforms the person's heart.

We should not only ask for forgiveness, but also receive it and believe in it. Sometimes we lack trust in it. Sometimes people say, "I've confessed that sin several times and I still don't feel forgiven!" That is a lack of faith. What does Scripture tell us?

I will remember their sin no more.[15]

Thou hast cast all my sins behind thy back.[16]

Why should we remember things when God has forgiven and forgotten them? We should never doubt God's

---

15. Jeremiah 31:34.
16. Isaiah 38:17.

forgiveness. On the psychological level, of course we may experience persistent painful memories; guilt feelings are difficult to get rid of completely. But the depths of our souls have been totally purified, and we can start again from zero, with full freedom and trust, as though nothing had happened. Thérèse wrote in a letter to Fr. Bellière:

> The memory of my faults humiliates me and leads me never to rely on my own strength, which is only weakness; but still more, the memory of them speaks to me of mercy and love. When, with filial trust, we throw our faults into the devouring furnace of love, how could they not be completely burned away?[17]

Finally, we come to perhaps the most beautiful stage of confession, the one Thérèse talked about in her parable of the two sons. After being deeply sorry for our sins, after asking for and receiving forgiveness and fulfilling the penance (normally a very light one) that the priest suggests to show our determination to change our ways, we thank our Lord and tell him, "Punish me with a kiss!" In other words, with a new outpouring of his love. Each confession is a little Pentecost, an outpouring of the Holy Spirit.

> I will sprinkle clean water upon you, and you will be clean from all your uncleannesses, and from all your

---

17. LT 247.

idols I will cleanse you. A new heart I will give you, and a new spirit I will put within you; and I will take out of your flesh the heart of stone and give you a heart of flesh.[18]

God promises an outpouring of the Holy Spirit who purifies us and gives us a heart capable of loving! This inner transformation is the fruit of the sacrament of reconciliation. What a pity it would be to deprive ourselves of it!

At the end of her last autobiographical manuscript, Thérèse wrote (in pencil, for she was exhausted by her sickness):

Yes, I feel that even though I had on my conscience all the sins that can be committed, I would go, heartbroken with repentance, to throw myself into Jesus' arms, because I know how dearly he loves the prodigal son who returns to him.[19]

Speaking to her sister, Mother Agnes, she added, to make sure the message got across:

People might think that it is because I have not sinned that I have such great trust in God. Tell them clearly, Mother, that if I had committed all possible crimes, I

18. Ezekiel 36:25–26.
19. ms C, 36 v°.

would still have the same trust. I feel that all that multitude of offenses would be like a drop of water falling into a blazing furnace.[20]

In other words: even if I had all the sins of the world on my conscience, I would maintain the same trust, because I trust in God, not my own deeds.

We should do all we can to avoid sin, and when aware of having sinned, we should tell God we are sorry and ask him to forgive us. To do that, it is good to go to confession regularly, at least once a month if possible. We should always do this with boundless trust in God's mercy. There are no limits to God's forgiveness.

We have spent a long time on the main aspects of Thérèse's little way: humility and trust. She talks about other attitudes that are also important. Let's look at them briefly.

A necessary expression of trust is self-abandonment.

Total abandonment: that is my only law.[21]

Jesus chose to show me the only path that leads to this divine furnace. That path is the abandonment of a little child who sleeps in his Father's arms without any fear.[22]

---

20. YN, July 11, 1897.
21. PN 32.
22. ms B, 1 r°.

The notion of abandonment includes "letting go" (not clinging to a particular project, a way of seeing things or acting, accepting that we can't control everything in our lives). It also includes relying on God, depending on him like a child. We should abandon ourselves into the hands of the All-Powerful no matter what the circumstances of our lives or the events we live through. Abandonment is one of the most beautiful ways of expressing our love. If we know someone loves us deeply and respects us, we find great happiness in abandoning ourselves totally to that person. We need to learn to abandon ourselves to God like that, in times of joy and also in difficult times.

At the end of Manuscript B, Thérèse says:

> I feel that if (which is impossible) you found a soul even weaker and smaller than me, you would be delighted to fill her with still greater favors, if she abandoned herself with total trust to your infinite mercy.[23]

Another important aspect of the spirituality of the little way is to live in the present moment. Not to go endlessly over the past, but leave it entirely to God and his mercy. Not to torment ourselves about tomorrow, but entrust it to his Providence.

The Gospel is very clear on this point.

---

23. ms B, 5 v°.

Therefore I tell you, do not be anxious about your life, what you shall eat or what you shall drink, nor about your body, what you shall put on . . . Which of you by being anxious can add one cubit to his span of life? . . . Your heavenly Father knows that you need them all.[24]

Worrying has never solved any problem. What solves problems are trust and faith.

Truly, I say to you, if you have faith as a grain of mustard seed, you will say to this mountain, "Move hence to yonder place," and it will move; and nothing will be impossible to you.[25]

Obviously this is just an image. But it is a pressing invitation to us to have more faith. Jesus says:

If God so clothes the grass of the field, which today is alive and tomorrow is thrown into the oven, will he not much more clothe you, O men of little faith?[26]

It's not that life has too many problems; it's that people lack faith. Yes, life isn't always easy. Sometimes it's really hard. We are often crushed and scandalized by things that happen in our own lives or those of others. But we need to face up to all that with faith and try to

---

24. Cf. Matthew 6:25–34.
25. Matthew 17:19.
26. Matthew 6:30.

live, day after day, trusting in the fact that God will keep his promises. Faith will lead us to salvation.

> Seek first his kingdom and his righteousness, and all these things shall be yours as well. Do not be anxious about tomorrow, for tomorrow will be anxious for itself. Let the day's own trouble be sufficient for the day.[27]

What does that mean? Let's try to live today as we should, according to the paths of the Kingdom, in trust and simplicity, seeking God and abandoning ourselves to him. And God will take care of the rest.

One day at a time. This is very important. Very often we exhaust ourselves going over the past again and again and also our fears about the future. But when we live in the present moment, we mysteriously find strength. We have the grace to live through what we encounter today. If tomorrow we must face more difficult situations, God will increase his grace. God's grace is given at the right time for it, day by day.

Sometimes we would like to lay in reserves, to stockpile strength for ourselves. But that isn't possible. Think of the image of the manna that fed the Israelites in the desert: if you tried to store it up, it spoiled.[28] God gave it daily, in the measure needed, neither more nor less;

---

27. Matthew 6:33–34.
28. Cf. Exodus 16:19–20.

and what's more, it tasted like whatever each person liked best. When we say the Our Father, we don't ask for large reserves (what would we do with them?), but simply the bread for today. And God gives it to us. We ought never to be anxious.

A Dominican priest once said to me, "What tires me out is not the work I do, it's the work I don't manage to do!" Often it's worrying that wears us out. By contrast, when we live in the present moment, in abandonment and trust in our Lord, we are given strength that enables us to live day by day, beginning again each morning. Forgetting the distance already traveled, as St. Paul says,[29] today we choose anew to believe, we choose to hope, we choose to love. And tomorrow we'll begin again, without getting upset. The spiritual life consists of that.

Living in the present moment means accepting the poverty in us: not insisting on going over and over the past or taking control of the future, but contenting ourselves with today. But this is very liberating. God does not dole out grace by a sort of profit-and-loss accounting of my past based on my good and bad actions. He gives me grace according to my faith today: "Be it done for you as you have believed!" The past doesn't matter. If today I make the decision to believe, to hope, and to love, I can

---

29. Cf. Philippians 3:13.

be certain of having all God's love to rely on. That is what happened to the good thief: "Today you will be with me in Paradise!"[30]

Another fundamental element of Thérèse's little way is love. "Love brings out love in return,"[31] she said, quoting St. John of the Cross. The love was already there, obviously, permeating all the attitudes we have talked about up till now—trust, humility, and abandonment. To those should be added all the little acts of love we choose to make in response to an invitation of the Spirit. These powerfully attract God's grace. What matters, as I said, is not to do extraordinary things, but for love to do the little things that form the fabric of our lives, to please God, to make our neighbors, parents, and friends happy. Thérèse called that "scattering flowers." We may prefer other terms, but we must not overlook this very valuable fact.

In this exercise of love, Thérèse lays great stress, especially at the end of her life, on fraternal love, love between those who are closest, the people we are in contact with every day. The surest way of loving God is loving the people around us—loving them in a considerate way, accepting them as they are. This is an essential point.

---

30. Luke 23:43.
31. ms C, 35 r°.

Surprisingly, right at the end of her life, in 1897, Thérèse made a rediscovery "of the mysterious depths of charity."[32] She wrote:

> This year, my dearest Mother, God has given me the grace to understand what charity is. Before, I understood it, it's true, but in an imperfect way. I had not plumbed the depths of Jesus' words: "The second commandment is like the first: You must love your neighbor as yourself."[33]

Until then, she had not fully understood how much Jesus was asking her to love the people she lived with every day, and the intrinsic connection between the first and the second commandment. It is relatively easy to love people who are far away, to pray for missionaries, etc. Loving those who are close to us is more difficult, but this is what the genuineness of our love for God will be judged on!

> Dearest Mother, upon meditating on these words of Jesus I understood how imperfect my love for my sisters was. I saw that I didn't love them as God loves them. Oh, now I understand that perfect charity consists of bearing with other people's faults, not being surprised

---

32. ms C, 18 v°.
33. ms C, 11 v°.

by their weaknesses, but being edified by the tiniest acts of virtue we see them practice. But above all, I have understood that charity must not be kept shut in the bottom of our hearts. Jesus says: "Men do not light a lamp and put it under a bushel, but on a stand, and it gives light to ALL in the house." It seems to me that this flame represents the charity that should give light and joy not only to those who are dearest to me, but to ALL in the house, without exception.

A very typical feature of Thérèse's "little way" is how she received the new commandment of charity, to love our neighbor as Jesus loves them. She perceived very clearly the demanding nature of this evangelical commandment, and how far beyond her capacity it was, but that did not discourage her. In fact, rather than a simple instruction, she understood this commandment of love as a wonderful promise. Jesus gives us what he asks us for: therefore he would come and do in her what was beyond her human possibilities.

O Lord, I know that you do not command anything impossible. You know my weakness and imperfection better than I do; you know that I could never love my sisters as you love them, if you, O my Jesus, did not love them in me too. It is because you want to grant me this grace that you have made a new commandment (cf. Jn 13: 24–25). O how I love it, since it gives me the assurance that your will is to love in me all those whom you command me to love!

This trust gave Thérèse the courage to set about loving the sisters whose life she shared through the vocation God had given her and never get discouraged. She sought to give all of them without exception a "spiritual banquet composed of friendly, joyful charity."[34] This means a thoughtful, sensitive, constant attention, especially toward people we don't feel any natural liking for, even though it sometimes seems difficult.

Manuscript C, containing her reflections on charity, and especially all the specific examples of it that she gives, is very necessary reading. These examples are of course drawn from her life in the Carmelite convent, her relationships with the other sisters, the novices in her charge, etc. But they can be applied to all sorts of family and community life. Here is an inexhaustible mine of very accurate and specific advice for all who want to learn to love their neighbor in line with the Gospel teachings.

This is all the more remarkable because at this period in her life Thérèse was going through a terrible dark night. She had no sense at all of God's presence and had strong temptations against faith and hope. Set against these was a sort of blossoming of charity, which seems extraordinary.

---

34. ms C, 28 v°.

This resembles the life of Mother Teresa of Calcutta, who, after the powerful graces that were at the origin of her vocation to the service of the poor, endured a state of great spiritual aridity. God suddenly seemed very far from her; however, she was intimately united to him in charity, while her faith and hope were plunged into darkness.

I consider this one of the little secrets of the spiritual life. In times when we are poor, dry, arid, with the feeling that God is far away, let's practice little works of love, especially in the area of fraternal charity, and we will find strength. Very often we recover our inner strength by forgetting ourselves in order to make life pleasant for others.[35]

I want to touch on one final point as an important element in Thérèse's little way (following the track we were on before, something that attracts God's grace, bringing his help into our lives).

I mean quite simply gratitude, being thankful. Let's read a passage from Thérèse on a lighter note that also contains a very profound truth. It isn't found in the *Complete Works* because it consists of some words recalled by her sister Celine (the fourth and last of the Martin sisters to enter Carmel, who took the name Sister Genevieve of the Holy

---

35. At the time of the grace she received at Christmas, Thérèse said: "I felt charity entering my heart, the need to forget myself in order to please others, and from then onwards I was happy." ms A, 45 v°.

Face), in a book called *Conseils et souvenirs* (translated into English in 1959 as *A Memoir of My Sister St. Thérèse*).

We have already considered some of the attitudes that attract God's grace (humility, trust, prayer, love). Thérèse mentions another in these words:

> What most attracts God's graces is gratitude, because if we thank him for a gift, he is touched and hastens to give us ten more, and if we thank him again with the same enthusiasm, what an incalculable multiplication of graces! I have experienced this: try it yourself and you will see! My gratitude for everything he gives me is limitless, and I prove it to him in a thousand ways.

I think these words contain a very deep and important truth. Saying thank you to God, being grateful for the good things he gives us, attracts new graces into our lives. It is not that they make God more generous, though we can see that God, being our Father, is moved by his children's gratitude and loves them still more for it. The point is that our gratitude does not "change" God, making him more generous, so to speak, but changes and purifies our hearts. "Blessed are the pure in heart, for they shall see God." They will see him in Paradise, of course, but here and now in this life they will see God's action, God's faithfulness.

I said before that among the things that purify our hearts are faith and trust. In the Acts of the Apostles, Peter speaks of the pagans, saying the Holy Spirit "cleansed their hearts by faith."[36] Another attitude that purifies our hearts thoroughly is gratitude. That's because it prevents us from getting tangled up in discouragement, sadness, withdrawal into ourselves, bitterness, dissatisfaction, discontent, etc.

Here we touch on something fundamental, unquestionably one of the secrets of the spiritual life that also is one of the laws of happiness. The more we cultivate gratitude and thanksgiving, the more open our hearts are to God's action, so that we can receive life from God and be transformed and enlarged. By contrast, if we bury ourselves in discontent, permanent dissatisfaction, then our hearts close themselves insidiously against life, against God's gift.

I know it isn't always easy to live in constant thanksgiving, but that is what Scripture invites us to do. "Give thanks in all circumstances; for this is the will of God in Christ Jesus for you,"[37] says St. Paul. Elsewhere, the Apostle says concisely and forcefully, "And be thankful!"[38] In other words, thanksgiving is not just a form of prayer to be practiced every Wednesday in a Charismatic Renewal meeting or every Sunday at Mass. It should be a way of

---

36. Acts 15:9.
37. I Thessalonians 5:18.
38. Colossians 3:15.

life. It is a life choice, a decision we make. When we are going through a time of trial, it obviously doesn't come spontaneously—that's quite understandable. We can't be always jumping for joy and clapping our hands. But we should still pay attention to this call from Scripture. And in so far as it depends on us, we should cultivate an attitude of thanksgiving, never letting slip an opportunity to say thank you to God, even for the tiniest things. Nor should we forget either to say thank you to other people, because it encourages them and deepens our communion with them.

The more we live in an atmosphere of gratitude, the more open our hearts are, and the more God can lead us and visit us. Thérèse understood this thoroughly and tried to practice it all the time, if only by making the effort to keep smiling.

We find this rather mysterious phrase in the Gospel: "For to him who has, more will be given, and he will have abundance; but from him who has not, even what he has will be taken away."[39] It can be understood this way: If you recognize what you have received, if you are grateful for the good and beautiful things already present in your life, you'll receive still more. But if you are always discontented and dissatisfied, you'll receive less and less. It is not God's fault, nor can you blame the hardness of your life; the

39. Matthew 13:12.

problem is that you shut yourself up in your discontent and resentment.

The question is how we choose to live our lives. The choice between discontent and gratitude is not the product of what we experience. It goes deeper. It's an appeal to the freedom we can always exercise.

This line of thought is important today. People have a strong tendency to shut themselves up in anxiety and fear, and also in a certain dissatisfaction (at least, in France the tendency is very strong). People are never satisfied with life, with the government, with each other; they always demand more, claim more rights, and accuse one another instead of living in trust and responsibility. Thus they shut themselves off in what soon becomes a vicious circle: the more discontented they are, the less they receive, and so they are still more unsatisfied. Here is a real "black hole" that swallows up all light!

This really is one of the basic laws of life. The more trust we have, the more we thank God for the way our lives are going, even if plenty of things aren't exactly as we would like, the more we will advance. If we give thanks for what we have already received, we will receive a lot more, and in the end we'll see our hearts being filled to overflowing.

Today, people often adopt a victim mentality. I'm unhappy, I don't have this, I don't have that, I've suffered, and it's all other people's fault. In the United States, the number of lawyers has grown enormously. People sue each other for anything and everything. Sometimes it is justified, but sometimes it is absurd. In France, a few years ago, a couple had a disabled baby; they couldn't accept the situation and tried to sue the doctor who'd done a prenatal test and hadn't seen the disability. They took the doctor to court, saying the birth of this disabled child had harmed the family and he was responsible. People lose common sense instead of welcoming life as it is, including the parts that are sometimes painful.

When we accept life as it is, with trust, it becomes good and beautiful, even in its difficult aspects. But if we're quick to complain and demand more rights, life becomes unlivable. It isn't God's fault or the fault of our lives; our inner attitude is destructive.

Conversely, faith, hope, love, and thanksgiving are remedies, counterweights, to the victim complex in which we sometimes are at risk of becoming entangled.

Little Thérèse made great efforts to live in that attitude of thanksgiving. She taught her novices to do the same. At a time when she was constantly being interrupted, she wrote: "I try to look happy, and above all, to be happy."[40] And she wrote to her sister Leonie: "The only happiness on this earth is to be determined always to find that what Jesus gives us is delightful."[41]

---

40. ms C, 17 v°.
41. LT 257.

From that perspective, she took after St. Teresa of Avila, who said she feared a discontented sister more than a swarm of devils!

Sometimes it requires heroic faith, but it's a very fruitful way of life and an excellent mode of spiritual training. If you are wondering what penance to take up next Lent, I suggest this one: try to be joyful, happy, and to thank God all the time. Nothing will do you as much good as that.

You might go so far as to say that when our hearts remain constantly in the act of thanksgiving, evil has no more hold on them. For in a grateful heart there is no longer any room for rancor, blame, unpleasantness, jealousy, and all the rest. Our hearts, remaining pure, are able to perceive God's action.

6.

ENDURING TRIALS

The point is often made that it's hard to keep one's trust in God while suffering. Jesus on the Cross pronounced the words, "My God, my God, why have you forsaken me?" Was that a lack of trust on his part?

No lack of trust, because Jesus' words are in fact the opening words of Psalm 21, which expresses great distress but ends on a magnificent note of hope:

> For God has not despised or abhorred the affliction of the afflicted; and he has not hidden his face from him, but has heard, when he cried to him. All the ends of the earth shall remember and turn to the Lord; and all the families of the nations shall worship before him!

Jesus indeed experienced in his humanity a terrible sense of being deserted by God. He chose to take upon himself the torment of all those who feel alone and abandoned. He wanted to experience all our sufferings, but in the certainty that God would intervene. Jesus' faith was tested to the limit, but he did not lose trust.

Similarly, though on a different level, little Thérèse's faith was also severely tested, especially in the last months of her life. But her trust remained intact. She explicitly understood this trial of suffering as a call to go to the extremes of trust. A few days before her death she said: "They" (her friends the saints) "want to see how far I am going to push my trust."[1]

Now I wish to move on to a second stage, which will be shorter. Having looked at the topic of trust in Thérèse of Lisieux, I want to tackle the following question: How can we face up to trials and suffering in our lives? We won't be taking little Thérèse as our explicit reference point, but I think we will be following her spirit faithfully.

To the question above, I obviously don't have any magic solution. But I would like to propose some very simple reflections, which can help provide guidelines.

First of all: don't be afraid. Let's not be afraid of life or difficulties or suffering. Obviously these things are not easy to face up to; they often leave us diminished and weakened. But they are part of life. We have to accept them, we have to "play the game," so to speak, full of

---

1. YN, September 22, 1897.

trust. "Everything is grace,"[2] said little Thérèse at the end of her life: everything can work together for our good, everything can be finally seen to be positive. To Dame Julian of Norwich, a medieval English mystic, Jesus said: "Thou shalt see thyself that all manner of things shall be well . . . I can make all things well."[3]

We can encounter all sorts of different trials in our lives: unemployment, health problems, marriage crises, the death of someone close to us, failures. . . . We can also go through depression, a dark night of the soul, crises in our relationship with God or in our vocation. There is a huge variety in this field. Luckily, all these things don't happen at once!

It's clear that different kinds of trials must be faced differently. Someone who suffers from depression is not in the same situation as someone who has lost a loved one. Each must be helped in a specific way, based on the nature and particular circumstances of his or her suffering.

That said, there are points common to all trials, and this is what I would like to look at now, because it may provide some light.

Every trial, no matter what its causes and characteristics are, is a trial of faith or of hope or of love. All three

2. YN, June 5, 1897.

3. Dame Julian of Norwich (1342–1416), *Revelations of Divine Love*, Chapter 32. According to Thomas Merton she was the greatest English theologian, along with Blessed John Henry Newman.

aspects usually are involved, with particular stress on one or the other.

Every trial is a trial of faith. If I am a believer and I am going through a difficult time, I will unavoidably ask myself at some stage, "What is God doing in all of this? Does he really love me? Is he present in what I am living through?" No matter whether it's sickness, unemployment, or something else, trust in God is put to the test, called into question; and to that question we always give, consciously or unconsciously, some answer.

We may doubt God's love, we may accuse him of abandoning us, we may rebel against him. These things often happen. However, it is possible—and this is beautiful and constructive—to see this time of trial as a call: a call to have a more determined, mature, and adult faith.

The specific question we are faced with—What is God doing? Is he really faithful? Can he draw good out of what is happening?—is simply a question of faith. We are invited to respond by deciding to have faith: "I believe! I continue to trust God! Even though I can't see, even though I don't feel anything, even though appearances are against it, I decide to believe. I will believe that God is faithful, that he will not let me fall, that he can draw something positive out of everything that is happening to me."

Trials are painful and mysterious; they have many aspects that cause scandal or are inexplicable, but they can also be understood as calls to make an act of faith, which then takes on immense value. Faith, says Scripture, is more precious than gold purified in the fire.[4]

Every trial is also a trial of hope. This is closely linked to what I've just said about faith, but there are some important points to add. When we are having a difficult time, one of the questions that comes up is this: In this painful experience, what do we rely on? What are we counting on? In what or in whom do we place our hope? How are we thinking of getting out of it? The answer we're invited to give is: I'm counting on the Lord, I'm expecting help from him. That doesn't mean I'm not going to apply all the human resources available, but at the deepest level I abandon myself into God's hands, and it is in him that I hope.

Another way of putting the question of hope is this: What is our security based on? When we go through a time of trial we become fragile. We are impoverished, having lost certain things we'd relied on before, such as good physical health. Or perhaps someone who was a support for us, whom we depended on, disappears or lets us down. Suddenly something has gone missing from among the things we counted on—our human possibilities, money,

---

4. Cf. I Peter 1:6–7: "You rejoice, though now for a little while you may have to suffer various trials, so that the genuineness of your faith, more precious than gold which though perishable is tested by fire, may redound to praise and glory and honor at the revelation of Jesus Christ."

friends, education, skills, qualifications, everything we normally depended on.

Finding ourselves poorer, we see more clearly the limitations of our human confidence. For instance, we may have been relying on a particular institution, and we find that it is defective. We had been idealizing our spouse or our community, and we realize that they are frail, that people are the same everywhere. Often in a trial this sense of fragility is especially painful. No longer do we know what to lean on, which saint to pray to. And the worst of it is that we can no longer rely on ourselves either, for we discover our own extreme fragility. We realize that we are more sinful than we thought, with less patience and less strength. We realize that we easily fall into anxiety, discouragement, and all the other negative feelings that can occur at such times.

The question therefore presents itself with particular urgency: Where have we placed our ultimate security? The answer we're invited to give is: My ultimate security is God. I rely on him alone.

Our only real security—and we have no other—is that God's mercy is unlimited. God is infinitely good and faithful. That is our only rock, to use the very concrete language of Scripture. All the rest—health, education, qualifications, friends, our own strength, our virtues— can leave us. We must be realistic! All those things are of course very good. A certain income, emotional security, faithful friends, a spiritual companion, good education, plenty of experience, a community we're happy to belong to, and so on: all those are valuable things. We should welcome them and seek them insofar as we can, but we should never make them our security. For God alone is absolute security. All the rest is relative. That is a fundamental point about trials of hope: we may experience a certain impoverishment, fragility in certain areas, precisely so that we learn to find our true security more fully in God. And God can never forsake us. Scripture says this endlessly:

> For the mountains may depart and the hills be removed,
> but my steadfast love shall not depart from you, and my
> covenant of peace shall not be removed, says the Lord,
> who has compassion on you.[5]

The sense of insecurity and fragility that we often experience in trials is admittedly very unpleasant and can produce a kind of panic, but it is also an opportunity: a call to become more firmly rooted in God. As an expression found so often in the Bible puts it: "He only is my rock and my salvation, my fortress, I shall not be shaken."[6] That will give us true freedom in the end.

Thirdly, every trial is a trial of love. Perhaps our relationship with God is in crisis or perhaps our relationship

5. Isaiah 54:10.
6. Psalm 61:6.

with our neighbor (in our marriage, for instance). But often the difficulty also concerns our relationship with ourselves, our love for ourselves.

For example, sometimes we may lose a taste for prayer. What does that trial mean? It is a call to continue praying all the same, because we don't pray just because we enjoy it or experience satisfaction, but first and foremost to please God. When we find great pleasure in it, that's fine, but when prayer is difficult, we need to keep going just the same! That purifies our love for God, which becomes freer, more disinterested, more genuine, and not just a selfish search for ourselves.

It's similar in what concerns our relationship with our neighbor. You loved your wife when she was young, pretty, well-behaved, pleasant, and answered all your expectations. Now you notice that she is sometimes bad-tempered, that she has a few wrinkles; do you continue to love her? Do you love her for yourself or do you love her truly, with a love that consists of wanting her good, and not only seeking your own satisfaction?

We are constantly faced with this kind of trial in which we confront the demands of loving another person as he or she is, loving them freely and disinterestedly, forgiving them, etc.

But sometimes our love for ourselves is called into question. We saw this before: you loved yourself when you were satisfied with yourself, when everything was going well, but now, seeing your inner poverty and sinfulness, you begin to hate yourself. No! Accept yourself in all your poverty and limitations.

I could cite endless examples showing that in every trial there is also a certain purification of love: love for God, love for ourselves, or love for our neighbor. It's not to destroy love, but so that love becomes deeper, truer, more evangelical and, basically, happier. We should not be afraid of crises. Today, for instance, as soon as a married couple hits a crisis, they separate, and each looks for someone new. How sad! Perhaps that crisis was the very opportunity they needed to deepen their relationship and adjust things to make their love truer. Every crisis is a chance to grow, an invitation to undertake a certain kind of work on ourselves.

The conclusion of these reflections is that in every trial it is essential to ask oneself a question along these lines: What act of faith am I being invited to make in this situation? What attitude of hope am I being called to live by? And what conversion in relation to love, leading to a love that is truer and purer, am I being summoned to undertake?

If we ask ourselves these questions honestly, we'll always find an answer. We'll discover some kind of call from God at the heart of our trial, and that will give it meaning.

What enables us to overcome a trial is not a magic wand that solves everything, but the discovery of what call it is that's being addressed to us, how we're being asked to grow. In understanding and responding to that call, we find new strength, enabling us to get through the trial and make something positive of it. Every trial can become a path of life, for Christ has risen from the dead and is present everywhere, sowing the seeds of new life in every situation. Even in those that seem most negative and most desperate, God is present.

On the basis of that principle, let's ask ourselves what is necessary in practice to "make it work," so to speak. What attitudes do we need to be able to move forward positively through a trial?

First, we must accept it. As long as we rebel, rejecting the situation in which we find ourselves, we won't be able to go forward. We need to say yes. That can take time, and it's normal that it should. Sometimes years are required to accept a death or a serious sickness. But we must set off on this path of acceptance, which isn't fatalism or resignation but an act of consent. Trusting God, I trust life.

Next (even though there's no rigid chronological order that must be followed and all sorts of variations are possible), we need to ask ourselves the right questions.

In a time of trial, a thousand questions can arise. Why has this happened to me? What did I do wrong to deserve this? What mistake did I make? (Sometimes people say, "What did I do to God to deserve this suffering?") What's the explanation of it all? What's causing it? How long will it go on? What's the quickest way out? Is this the way it usually happens? For instance, is it normal for someone who's always been faithful to God to suffer from depression? One of the commonest questions is, Whose fault is it—my own or other people's? Who is to blame?

We ask ourselves huge numbers of questions, often with great pain and anguish. That's inevitable. But one must look carefully at one's attitude in all this questioning, especially when the question is, "Who is to blame for what's happening to me?"

Certain primary psychological mechanisms operate very quickly and quite dangerously. We dislike suffering, obviously, and it is normal that we want to end it. So first we try and identify its cause, easily persuading ourselves that when we've learned who is responsible, we can eliminate the suffering. Everyone who suffers seeks someone to blame. Thus suffering very easily leads to accusation. We accuse God, we accuse life, we accuse other people, and sometimes we accuse ourselves, indulging in unjustifiable blame and guilt.

We must be very watchful here. Although it's normal in suffering to look for causes and remedies, we must take care to keep our hearts pure. Making accusations and seeking scapegoats is a constant temptation in social life. Not finding a scapegoat, people invent one, as Hitler did in making the Jews scapegoats for all the problems of Germany. Don't be naive; we're subject to the same temptations today. A society in crisis will always try to identify some group of people to blame for its problems.

We need to give this point close attention in regard to our personal lives. Vigilance is required to ensure that suffering doesn't turn into bitterness, blame, and constant mutual recriminations. . . . People often go that route, but it doesn't solve anything.

The questions we ask in times of trial, including those I've mentioned, are perfectly justifiable. Sometimes there's even an answer. The cause of some suffering may be identified or the person responsible located, and the remedy discovered in this way.

But justifiable as the questions may be, there isn't always an answer. And it's very common for people to get irretrievably tangled up in them and end up going round and round in circles.

Take the question "Why?" Why is this happening to me? Most of the time there's no answer, or at least no immediate one. Perhaps we'll understand in ten or twenty years, but just now there's no answer, and we risk shutting ourselves up inside our need for one—forever demanding an explanation that doesn't exist. Not everything in life can be explained to human satisfaction. And the more we demand an explanation without finding one, the more frustrated we become, the more bitter and filled with blame. You sometimes see people trap themselves in this way in a sort of vicious circle.

Similarly, we can also go round and round in an endless search for someone to blame for our misfortunes. Some painful situations are too complex and mixed-up for it to be possible to identify any one person as the one at fault. We need to have the wisdom to admit this.

Keep this clearly in mind, then: the questions we've been looking at are normal, but they don't always have clear answers and we can get fruitlessly bogged down in looking for these. When we realize that's happening—that we're going round and round and getting nowhere, that our questions aren't producing light but only bitterness and blame—we must have the courage to put those questions aside and ask ourselves another. It's the only essential one, after all, and it will always be answered: What attitude does God want me to have toward this situation?

The point is to move from "Why?" to "How?" The real question isn't "Why is this happening to me?" but "How should I live through these things?" How am I called to face this situation? What call to growth is being made to me through this? That question will always get an answer.

Allow me to underline what I'm saying. In difficult times we want all possible explanations for what's happening to us. But this search for explanations isn't always as pure as it may seem. Part of it is quite justifiable: seeking the truth, seeking solutions to problems, etc. But mixed up with this one very often finds other motives that aren't right. Sometimes we seek answers out of simple curiosity; sometimes to find people we can blame, on whom we can unload our share of the responsibility. Sometimes, too, we insist on having an answer in order to reassure ourselves or set our minds at rest. Our security depends on having answers that our minds can handle, that our capacity for understanding situations can take in. But this isn't the real basis of our security: that basis is God. Knowing and understanding everything can't save us. That's a very common illusion, but it isn't knowledge that saves: it is faith and trust.

It's right and necessary to ask questions, but sometimes we should also ask ourselves what our questions really mean! In this life it is sometimes absolutely necessary that we consent to go forward without understanding. The purification and refining of our minds and our perception of reality depends on this. There are times when we are called to believe, even if we don't understand. "Blessed are those who have not seen, and yet believe!"[7]

Ultimately, the only real questions in our lives are those whose answer lead us to personal conversion, to progress in love. You can see that very clearly today when the media flood us with information. It sometimes seems as if the better informed people are, the less able they are to find answers to their real questions!

---

7. John 20:29.

Let me offer some practical advice. When preoccupied with a question to which you can't find the answer, ask yourself: Do I absolutely need an answer to that question in order to know how I should live my life today? You'll realize that usually you don't. So you can set the question aside for the time being without any harm, and it will simplify your life. I'm firmly convinced that when we have a question to which we need to know the answer in order to do God's will today, he always responds.

Sometimes we go over and over our questions. Then we must have a "Copernican revolution," so to speak, and change our approach. Instead of insisting on answers to all our questions, we resolve to accept the partial darkness and ask ourselves the real question. We accept the situation as it is, without aiming to understand it entirely, and ask: What does God want of me here? What is the right way to live through this? Which part of the Gospel am I called by this situation to put into practice now? What acts of faith and hope, what progress in love, am I being asked to make today? What good can be accomplished in this situation that depends on me? Without fretting any more about what other people should do or should have done, we look to our own responsibilities: What good, depending on me, can I do today that nobody else can do?

All these are in fact the same question. And it always has an answer. Even in the worst situations, in face of the most traumatic injustices, we can discover a good to be accomplished, a step to be taken in our personal progress, and ultimately that's what counts. The light appears little by little, and a very important condition for that to happen is living in the present moment. We shouldn't demand a final answer for the long term, but accept that sometimes light is given to us "just for today" (the refrain of a poem by Thérèse).[8] If we demand long-term answers, we won't always get them. We have to consent to live from day to day, take one step at a time, without necessarily knowing what the next will be.

The results are very beneficial. First, meaning is restored to what we are living through. Before, we felt everything was absurd and chaotic. Now we are aware of a call we can respond to—we can act, make choices, move forward. Things begin to make sense again. Perhaps it's only for now and not for the next fifty years, but that doesn't matter. Day by day, we understand which direction to go in, which call to answer. Our lives recover meaning and orientation, our peace of soul is restored, as well as a certain confidence in the future.

Another very beneficial result is that we drop the victim attitude and assume an attitude of responsibility.

8. PN 5.

We stop looking for people to blame and accusing others, and shoulder our own lives again. And having assumed responsibility, we can do the good that depends on us.

At the same time, we recover interior strength. There are two reasons for that: a psychological one and a spiritual one. On the psychological level, we regain strength because we know where to focus our efforts. Before, we were troubled by a thousand questions, wearing ourselves out, not knowing what to concentrate on; but now we know what we should do and can focus on that. Above all—and this is the spiritual reason—every time we respond to a call from God, we receive grace and are interiorly strengthened. Because God is faithful: if he asks us to take this or that step forward, he comes to the aid of our weakness. We are still little and fragile, but we receive a certain courage that enables us to go forward. God supports our steps.

Plus we recover our self-respect and a certain self-confidence. Before, we spent time complaining or lamenting, but now we have again shouldered responsibility for our lives, and that reconciles us to ourselves. We must realize that nothing is more destructive of our self-confidence than seeing ourselves as permanent victims. Here, of course, I'm talking about the false victim complex of people who entangle themselves in wailing and blame instead of shouldering their responsibilities. Some people really are victims of injustice, and it's entirely healthy for them to admit it. A child who has been sexually abused may feel guilty about it because he can't see where the real responsibility lies. He needs to be told: You aren't guilty, you're the victim. That liberates him, because it's the truth. But there are also many false ways in which people see themselves as victims.

The path that I have outlined (acceptance of the painful situation, changing the approach of our questions, consenting to take just one step at a time, and discovering the answer as it gradually appears) demands courage, but in the end it is very positive.

This process may take time; we may advance quickly or slowly, and we must be patient. We need patience toward other people and toward ourselves. When someone is suffering, you can't just tell them, "You should do this" or "You must do that." A lot of thought and care is needed to accompany them spiritually.

Simply helping someone accept his or her situation can take a long time. We need to help the person work toward acceptance, knowing a plant can't be made to grow by pulling it. We have to accompany this individual step after step, at the right pace. We must help him or her not become shut up in their suffering, bitterness, fears, or false questions, by inviting the person to trust. But it's the person involved who will know when he or she can truly say yes. We can't say yes for that individual or compel him to say yes before the time is right and his heart is open to hope. That takes understanding and perceptiveness—allowing time to express emotions and calm down; we can't try to go faster than the Holy Spirit. But what I've said offers pointers, first for ourselves and also in accompanying other people.

In sum, faced with trials we shouldn't be afraid. We should accept things as they come, even if that isn't how we expected our lives to unfold. Let's try to discern, within that trial, the calls being made to us, the conversions being suggested, and then we will find the grace to live through them. That is the attitude that turns hard events into something positive in the end and enables us to grow in all circumstances.

I've outlined some general principles. Each of us individually must see how to apply them in particular cases. Taking them into consideration may be a very liberating experience.

The path I propose here isn't magic. It demands a program of work on ourselves, but that's how we can go forward. I think little Thérèse would be in total agreement with what I've just suggested. She experienced great trials in her life but was always able to accept them and try to understand what God was asking of her through them.

There was a wonderful example of this at the end of her life. For about a year and a half before her death, Thérèse lived in the deepest interior darkness. She had always taken enormous joy in thinking of heaven and the happiness that was to come, and in believing in Jesus. But from Easter 1896,[9] everything became difficult and dark for her.

> Jesus has permitted my soul to be invaded by the deepest darkness, and that the thought of Heaven, that had always been so sweet to me, should bring me nothing but struggle and torment.[10]

She never lost her faith, but faith itself became a painful struggle. She said:

> When (in my poems) I sing of the happiness of Heaven . . . I feel no joy in it at all, for I am only singing of what I <u>want to believe</u>.

She wrote out the Creed in her blood and carried it next to her heart. She was assailed by doubts and temptations of every kind: God does not exist, everything you've believed and rejoiced in is nothing but an illusion; after death you will fall into nothingness; science holds the explanation for everything, etc. It was a very painful fight, but fight she did! What's very moving is the meaning all this took on for her. She accepted it as a purification of whatever elements of her hope in heaven might be overly human[11] and, above all, as an invitation to pray for atheists.

---

9. See ms C, 5 v°.

10. ms C, 5 v°.

11. "It took away any kind of natural satisfaction that I may have had in my desire for Heaven." ms C, 7 r°.

She lived in a time when triumphalist atheism was flourishing and very sure of itself. Many people really thought religion was finished and science had taken its place and would provide the explanation for everything. Science, it was thought, had all the answers, and the happiness of mankind would be the necessary result of scientific progress. All the great illusions of late nineteenth-century atheism! Thérèse sensed that she was being called to offer up her sufferings for all who had no faith. She said:

> Your child asks you for forgiveness for her brothers, and she consents to eat the bread of sorrow for as long as you wish, and will not leave the table heaped with bitterness at which poor sinners eat, before the day you shall appoint. . . . May all those who are not yet enlightened by the radiant torch of Faith finally see it shining.

Speaking of her dryness and darkness in prayer some years before in one of her letters to Celine, she had already said, "May my darkness serve to enlighten other souls!"[12] In other words: I accept being in darkness, I have faith and that is enough for me. I don't need proofs, I don't need ecstasies, faith is enough for me; I accept this "subterranean darkness"[13] in which I am plunged, asking God to enlighten others who don't have the grace of faith or who refuse it.

---

12. LT 102.
13. Ibid.

Every trial can have a meaning, but we can't invent one for it; we can't place made-up labels on things from the outside. Sometimes we're too quick and too superficial in interpreting events. It doesn't help people to say, "If you're undergoing this trial, it's because God wants to tell you this or is asking you to do that . . . ."

There are examples of that attitude in the book of Job. Job was enduring a time of terrible trial, having lost absolutely everything. His friends came to talk to him with the aim of helping, but they did exactly the opposite. This was the sort of thing they said: "If you're having this trial, it's because you must have committed a sin at some stage. Look carefully at your life and you will find a fault you have committed somewhere . . . ." Job rejected this interpretation, and he was quite right. We should be very careful about any interpretative scenarios we devise— especially if they seem very spiritual to us! Otherwise, the result will be that, like Job's friends, instead of giving good advice we will only discourage people even more.

So we should not supply ready-made answers, based on wonderfully spiritual theories of our own. When people are undergoing trials, we should try to help them discover for themselves God's specific call, the path that is opening up before them. The meaning of a trial will never consist of a general explanation of the situation. The path opens up little by little, step by step. We need to help people to clear the way, not shut themselves up in their bitterness or accusations but discover for themselves how to go forward, what choices to make for their lives. It is not always easy. Sometimes I've spoken for hours with someone in rebellion without succeeding in getting them to look on their situation with renewed hope. We just have to accept our powerlessness. All we can do for someone may be to pray, keep silence, and hope for them. We don't always have the right arguments to persuade them or the right light to help them, and we must accept our own poverty there too while allowing the other person to find his or her own way.

One other point. When God permits trials in our lives, I think it's also to help us understand others better and find the best words to help them. Not with some theory we've invented, but by having the right attitude and words to support and console them. To really support and console others, we need to accept trials and difficulties ourselves, so that we can understand things from the inside and not just in the abstract.

These are obviously complex questions whose proper discussion would take much more time. I hope anyway that what I've said may help someone.

In any case, let's never lose trust. I said earlier that the right question to ask in a time of trial, the one that really helps us go forward, is: "What act of faith am I being called to make, what attitude of trust am I being called to adopt, what conversion to love am I being called to undertake?" The order of the terms is important. We must begin with faith and trust. For if we set out with a disposition of faith and trust, we will also have the light to see what conversion we are called to with regard to love. As long as we walk in faith and trust, we will know the path. But if we lose trust and faith, everything goes dark—we lose clear vision and the capacity for discernment. So ultimately, the real battle is to persevere in faith and trust, or to recover them. Then we'll also be able to see what progress is possible in love. We must take things in that order.

Finally, let's ask our Lord to help us have the courage to believe, and always to be able to look at ourselves, the world and the Church with hope. It is by keeping, or recovering, that hope-filled outlook that we will be able to help the people whom God places along our way. Let's also ask our Lord to purify our love, to make it truer, deeper, and ultimately happier.

What I am setting out for us all is a demanding path, a path of responsibility, one that requires us to be adults in the spiritual sphere. But it is the path of life and joy.